THE TRANSFORMATION OF THE AMERICAN ECONOMY, 1865-1914

AN ESSAY IN INTERPRETATION

THE TRANSFORMATION OF THE AMERICAN ECONOMY, 1865-1914

AN ESSAY IN INTERPRETATION

ROBERT HIGGS
UNIVERSITY OF WASHINGTON

LvMI
MISES INSTITUTE

TO DAYL AND MATTHEW

With Love

Ludwig von Mises Institute
518 West Magnolia Avenue
Auburn, Alabama 36832 U.S.A.
mises.org

ISBN 978-1-61016-240-1

PREFACE TO THE 2011 EDITION

This book, my first, was composed for the most part in 1969 and 1970 and published in 1971, exactly forty years ago. At that time, I was in my mid-twenties and had just completed my work for the Ph.D. degree in economics at the Johns Hopkins University. At Hopkins, I had been trained entirely along the lines of the neoclassical synthesis that, at that time, reigned supreme in the best U.S. universities. This approach to economic analysis rests on a positivistic epistemological foundation: theory serves as a source of empirically testable hypotheses and, in the event that the data do not refute the hypotheses, as a framework for understanding the empirical observations. This methodological understanding was not so much taught as presumed, and students absorbed it by osmosis from their teachers and from the articles and books their professors assigned.

The arguments presented in this book rest explicitly on such an approach. Indeed, its young author carries water for neoclassical economics proudly, with no signs of any misgiving about the approach as such, but only cautions about its misapplication or about unwarranted conclusions derived from it. Even at a tender age, I had learned to be careful about the data used in empirical tests and to take care not to claim too much for the conclusions reached in such analysis. Yet, at that time, I entertained no doubts—indeed, my teachers had never given me any reason for doubt—about the correctness of this way of doing economic analysis.

Hence, the book brims with statements about theories from which testable hypotheses may be derived and about the tests conducted to determine whether the data refute the hypotheses and therefore call into question the underlying theory, or "model." Although the book presents hardly any formal econometrics, much of its content represents my translation of formal econometric findings into language understandable by readers untrained in economic theory and statistical inference.

When the book was composed, the so-called New Economic History, or cliometrics, was riding high among academic economic historians, and I was proud to go forth as one of the young knights doing battle in the crusade to remake the study of economic history along more scientific lines—to make economic history not the poor stepchild of economics, as it had long been, but a field of applied economics fully entitled to stand alongside other well-established fields, such as labor economics, public finance, and international trade. We cliometricians sought to correct the many errors committed over the years by historians untrained in economics. Although, to be sure, many such errors cried out for correction, I later came to see in retrospect that we were much too full of ourselves and that we—certainly I—still had much to learn about many things.

As soon as I began my academic career, I started to learn these lessons. In part, this self-education took the form of learning how to work as a more skillful craftsman in the cliometric workshop. But in another part my learning carried me on a long journey away from my initial training in and commitment to the positivistic epistemological foundation of neoclassical economics. Indeed, I would eventually conclude that my initial acceptance of this approach was a mistake, and I would come to see the methodological practice of mainstream, neoclassical analysis not as a form of science, but as a form of scientism—a misapplication of methods suitable for studying material nature but unsuitable for studying human action. My journey away from neoclassical epistemology began with my reading of works by F.A. Hayek, which in due course led me to works by Ludwig von Mises and other economists writing in the Austrian tradition. Here I discovered an approach to economic analysis that I found far more convincing than the one I had followed in the early years of my career.

So, reading through my *Transformation of the American Economy* after forty years, I have the eerie feeling that despite its familiarity, it was written by someone else. I no longer stand by the book's methodological pronouncements or by much of what it represents as "modern economic theory." Yet, I do not want to apologize too much. A great deal of the economic analysis still seems sound to me; after all, in the area known as applied microeconomics, the neoclassicals and the Austrians hold similar views in regard to their basic understanding of how many actions and events are interrelated. And even in regard to the econometrics on which I relied for the first fifteen or twenty years of my career, I have come to believe that not all of my work (and others' work along similar lines) was for naught. I now believe, however, that inferential statistics—econometric "tests of hypotheses"—have no defensible place in economics or the other human sciences. However, if one views the econometric findings not as a means of making inferences in testing hypotheses, but simply as descriptive statistics, one may make valuable use of such findings in writing economic history. I urge the reader to understand the book's presentation in this light.

ROBERT HIGGS
August 2011

PREFACE

This book offers an interpretation of American economic development in the half century after the Civil War. Its hypotheses are drawn from modern economic theory, and the evidence presented is largely statistical; but the book is written in plain English, and the reader needs no previous training in economics or statistics to comprehend it. Chapter I furnishes a brief survey of the analytical framework; more detailed theoretical discussions appear at appropriate places in the subsequent chapters. Included are many subjects that have just begun to receive rigorous historical study—for example, health improvements, racial discrimination, invention, and urban growth—as well as some that are customarily treated in the textbooks. Although parts of the book do nothing more than "translate" the recent historical research of economists into language comprehensible to the general reader, I have in several instances attempted to push out the frontiers of knowledge and to raise questions for future research. I hope therefore that the book will interest my fellow economic historians as well as provide a useful analysis for students and general readers.

The central feature of the 1865–1914 era in American economic history was economic growth—a rapid and sustained rise in output per capita that constituted the return on investments in health, skills, and knowledge as well as investments in buildings, machines, and inventories. Inextricably related to economic growth was the transformation of the economy's structure—most importantly, the relative decline of agricultural output and employment and the concomitant rise of urban manufacturing, trade, and service industries, often described as an "industrial revolution." Institutions in general, and property rights in particular, were of critical importance in determining the rate of economic growth; conversely, growth gave rise to changes in institutions. Chapters II–IV focus on growth, transformation, and institutional change. Chapter V deals with questions of inequality in the distribution of income and wealth.

This small volume makes no pretense of comprehensiveness. Many traditional subjects do not appear at all, and others receive only cursory attention—treatment that tells the reader something about what I consider relatively unimportant. Because my main interest is interpretation, I have included only enough detail to make the book self-contained. A rather lengthy bibliography gives the sources of more detailed description and analysis. I hope that the book's brevity will be considered a virtue but, like any short treatment of a broad subject, my comments tread a thin line between clarifying the issues and oversimplifying them. As a warning against overstepping this line, I have occasionally employed footnotes to indicate that matters are not as simple as the text might suggest and to refer the reader to a fuller treatment. To keep the number of footnotes within tolerable bounds, I have refrained from documenting evidence available in the Census Bureau's well-known compilation, *Historical Statistics of the United States.*

Any merits of the book are attributable to many friends who generously assisted me. I wish to pay tribute to my teachers at The Johns Hopkins University—Edwin S. Mills, Peter Newman, Jürg Niehans, and H. Louis Stettler—who began the arduous task of making me an economist, and to my colleagues at the University of Washington, who are continuing the job. Also I am deeply indebted to those who read the manuscript and commented on it: Ralph L. Andreano, Mary L. Eysenbach, Dayl Higgs, Edward F. Meeker, Morris D. Morris, Nancy Neubert, Douglass C. North, Nathan Rosenberg, and David Sisk. Without belittling the others, I especially thank Professor North, for his unfailing encouragement, and Professor Rosenberg, whose incisive and wide-ranging comments contributed greatly toward improving the manuscript. Since I have stubbornly ignored much of their advice, none of the persons named should be held responsible in any way for the form or contents of the book.

ROBERT HIGGS

University of Washington, 1971

ACKNOWLEDGMENTS

Acknowledgment is due the publishers for their kind permission to print quotations or reproduce illustrations from the following works:

Allan G. Bogue, *Money at Interest: The Farm Mortgage on the Middle Border,* copyright © 1955. Ithaca, N. Y.: Cornell University Press.

Allan G. Bogue, *From Prairie to Corn Belt: Farming on the Illinois and Iowa Prairies in the Nineteenth Century,* copyright © 1963. Chicago: University of Chicago Press.

Alfred D. Chandler, Jr., *Strategy and Structure: Chapters in the History of the Industrial Enterprise,* copyright © 1962. Cambridge, Mass.: Massachusetts Institute of Technology Press.

Steven N. S. Cheung, "Private Property Rights and Sharecropping," *Journal of Poliltical Economy,* LXXVI (November/December 1968, copyright © 1968. Chicago: University of Chicago Press.

Steven N. S. Cheung, "Transaction Costs, Risk Aversion, and the Choice of Contractual Arrangements," *Journal of Law and Economics,* XII (April 1969), copyright © 1969 by The University of Chicago Law School. Chicago: University of Chicago Press.

Gilbert C. Fite, "Daydreams and Nightmares: The Late Nineteenth-Century Agricultural Frontier," *Agricultural History,* XL (October 1966), copyright © 1966 by The Agricultural History Society. Berkeley: University of California Press.

Robert William Fogel and Jack Rutner, "The Efficiency Effects of Federal Land Policy, 1850–1900: A Report of Some Provisional Findings," University of Chicago Center for Mathematical Studies in Business and Economics, Report 7027 (June 1970).

James Willard Hurst, *Law and the Conditions of Freedom in the Nineteenth-Century United States,* copyright © 1956 by Northwestern University. Madison: University of Wisconsin Press.

Eugene M. Lerner, "Southern Output and Agricultural Income, 1860–1880," *Agricultural History,* XXXIII (July 1959), copyright © 1959 by The Agricultural History Society. Berkeley: University of California Press.

W. Arthur Lewis, *The Theory of Economic Growth,* copyright © 1955. London: George Allen and Unwin, Ltd.

Richard G. Lipsy and Peter O. Steiner, *Economics,* copyright © 1966. New York: Harper and Row, Inc.

C. O. Paullin, in John K. Wright, Ed., *Atlas of the Historical Geography of the United States,* copyright © 1932. Washington, D. C.: Carnegie Institution of Washington.

Nathan Rosenberg, "Neglected Dimensions in the Analysis of Economic Change," *Bulletin of the Oxford University Institute of Economics and Statistics,* XXVI (February 1964), copyright © 1964. Oxford: Basil Blackwell and Mott, Ltd.

CONTENTS

LIST OF TABLES

LIST OF FIGURES

[O]bservations . . . are always *interpretations* of the facts observed . . . [and] they are *interpretations in the light of theories.*

KARL R. POPPER

INTRODUCTION: PROGRESS AND POVERTY

Some get an infinitely better and easier living, but others find it hard to get a living at all.

HENRY GEORGE

Building, wrecking, and rebuilding, with immense energy and boundless optimism, Americans in the half century after 1865 outstripped all rivals in the race to create wealth. But progress had its price. The creation of a modern, ever-expanding economy disrupted and then destroyed the old order in economic life, and casualties lay strewn along the road of progress. No one remained unaffected, nor did any industry or region escape the vast transformation that swept the nation. Men's reactions varied as widely as the events themselves. Some, their own fortunes swept along with the general upsurge, rejoiced in the economy's development, while others, caught in the backwaters of progress, lamented the losses and disappointments that unanticipated changes had imposed on them. By examining the effects of this great transformation on particular men, industries, and regions, we can begin to grasp their extent, to appreciate their bewildering variety. These introductory pages present a few illustrations.

To millions of downtrodden Europeans, America was the land of promise. Seeking that promise, William Carnegie, a hand weaver displaced by machinery, left Scotland with his family in 1848 for the United States. Like many other immigrants, however, he found the promise illusory, and his son Andrew, aged 13, went to work in a textile mill at $1.20 a week to help support the family. Many years later Andrew recalled: " It was a hard life. In the winter father and I had to rise and breakfast in the darkness, reach the factory before it was daylight, and, with a short interval for lunch, work till after dark. The hours hung heavily upon me and in the work itself I took no pleasure." During the years that followed, as a messenger boy, a telegraph operator, a railroad superintendent, and finally an independent businessman of diversified interests, he advanced until in the early 1870's, already moderately wealthy, he made a fateful decision: "I would concentrate on the manufacture of iron and steel and be master in that." The decision proved wise. For the next 30 years the rise of Carnegie paralleled the spectacular rise of the American iron and steel industry. His fortune mounted steadily, and in 1901 he finally sold the business for over $225 million and "resolved to stop accumulating and begin the infinitely more serious and difficult task of wise distribution." One of the world's richest men, he spent the last 18 years of his life giving away his wealth to promote various humanitarian organizations, many of his own creation. It seemed that America was, after all, really the land of promise.[1]

While Carnegie concentrated his energies on iron and steel, others supposed that a farm in the West offered an opportunity for material success. In ignorance of the true risks, many committed themselves to failure. Writing to the state governor in 1874, a Minnesota girl, Jennie Flint, described her family's condition:

> We have no money now nothing to sell to get any more clothes with as the grasshoppers destroyed all of our crops what few we had for we have not much land broke yet; as we have no team of our own we have to hire one in order to get it worked what little we have to sow, so you see it is rather hard on us to hire so much and get along. We managed to raise a few potatoes and some corn and a little buckwheat and that is all we have to depend upon. We are very bad off for bedding not having but two quilts and two sheets in the house and have to make them serve two beds. We have to use our clothing, that we wear, on the beds to keep us from suffering with the cold and then it [is] most impossible to keep warm for our house is so open . . . . We have not got our house plastered as yet only on the outside with mud could not get any lime to do it with for we had no money nor could not get any, almost perish here sometimes with the cold . . . . Now if you will be so kind as to send us some bedding and clothes and yarn to knit us some stockings with we have no wool nor yarn. Or send us some money so we can get them ourselves, we would be thankful . . . .

[1] Andrew Carnegie, *Autobiography of Andrew Carnegie* (Boston: Houghton-Mifflin, 1920), pp. 34, 177, 255.

Twenty years later, a Kansas housewife, Mrs. Susan Orcutt, wrote to her state's governor:

I take my pen in hand to let you know that we are starving to death. It is pretty hard to do without anything to eat here in this God forsaken country . . . . My husband went away to find work and came home last night and told me that we would have to starve . . . . It is pretty hard for a woman to do without anything to eat when she doesn't know what minute she will be confined to bed. If I was in Iowa I would be all right . . . . I haven't had nothing to eat today and it is 3 o'clock.[2]

Not everyone, it seems, shared equally in the fruits of progress.

While the fortunes of individuals differed dramatically, the development of different industries varied no less. Some expanded by leaps and bounds, steel being perhaps the best example. In 1886 a leading financial newspaper reported:

New steel plants are being put up in all sections of the country. In the Bulletin of the Steel Association for February 10, 1886, we find no less than 13 works for the manufacture of Bessemer steel that have either recently been completed or are in process of construction and expect to be in operation some time in the present year. These new works are going up in a great many different States—Pennsylvania, New York, New Jersey, Ohio, Illinois, West Virginia—and it is true, as the Bulletin says, that the Bessemer steel industry is no longer confined to a few establishments located in three or four States.[3]

And despite such enormous additions to supply, the demand for steel expanded so rapidly that entrepreneurial returns remained high, making millionaires of Carnegie and many other steel producers.

Not every industry yielded such returns, however, and agriculture in particular seemed unable to keep pace. Writing in 1891, Rodney Welch gave an account with which many farmers surely agreed:

I doubt if farmers are any better contented with their lot, or if they obtain more enjoyment from life, than they did in old times. I also question if they are more prosperous. They are generally in a condition of unrest, if not of discontent. Their social condition has not improved, as has that of mechanics and traders. Most of them are anxious to leave the farm for the store, the shop, the mine, or the locomotive. . . . Farmers have long been losing their place and influence in the councils of the State and nation. Our later Congresses have not contained enough farmers from the northern

[2] Both letters as cited in Gilbert C. Fite, "Daydreams and Nightmares: The Late Nineteenth-Century Agricultural Frontier," *Agricultural History*, XL (Oct. 1966), 289, 292.

[3] *Commercial and Financial Chronicle*, XLII (Feb. 13, 1886), 199.

> States to constitute the committees on agriculture. Our national law-makers have known so little about what would promote the prosperity of farmers that they have favored measures that have greatly injured agriculture. . . . [T]he price of nearly every farm product has declined sometimes below the cost of the labor required to produce it.[4]

Sharply contrasting changes not only occurred among individuals and industries but had a geographic dimension as well; whole regions developed quite differently. In 1869, the hamlet of Wichita, Kansas, boasted four shops, a blacksmithy, a saddlery, a saloon, and 20 families betting on the future of the little place. It proved a good bet. By 1880 Wichita's population had expanded to 5000, by 1890 to 24,000. And such growth occurred commonly in that booming part of the country. During the same period, for example, Omaha grew from 16,000 to 149,000, Kansas City from 35,000 to 176,000, and hundreds of new towns sprang up west of the Mississippi.[5]

Elsewhere the scene differed markedly. On a trip through southern Vermont in the 1880's Charles Nott observed:

> Midway between Williamstown and Brattleboro . . . I saw on the summit of a hill against the evening sky what seemed a large cathedral. Driving thither, I found a huge, old-time, two-story church, a large academy (which had blended in the distance with the church), a village with a broad street, perhaps 150 feet in width. I drove on and found that the church was abandoned, the academy dismantled, the village deserted. The farmer who owned the farm on the north of the village lived on one side of the broad street, and he who owned the farm on the south lived on the other, and they were the only inhabitants. All of the others had gone—to the manufacturing villages, to the great cities, to the West. Here had been industry, education, religion, comfort, and contentment, but there remained only a drear solitude of forsaken homes.[6]

And the story could have been repeated, with minor variations, for scores of other villages across northern New England.[7]

[4] Rodney Welch, "The Farmer's Changed Condition," *The Forum*, X (1891), 695, 699.

[5] Constance McLaughlin Green, *American Cities in the Growth of the Nation* (New York: Harper Colophon Books, 1965), pp. 148-66; Robert Higgs, "The Growth of Cities in a Midwestern Region, 1870–1900," *Journal of Regional Science*, IX (Dec. 1969), 369–70.

[6] Charles C. Nott, "A Good Farm for Nothing," *The Nation*, XLIX (Nov. 21, 1889), 406.

[7] Harold Fisher Wilson, *The Hill Country of Northern New England: Its Social and Economic History, 1790–1930* (New York: Columbia University, 1936), pp. 97–115.

We could continue to pile fact upon fact, but such efforts alone would certainly generate as much confusion as understanding. How can we see all these facts as parts of an overall pattern and relate them to one another in sequences of cause and effect? In short, how can we understand them?

I

MAKING SENSE OF THE FACTS

[T]he simplifications of an analytical method furnish a powerful tool for understanding some of the fundamental controlling interrelationships in historical change. That such a technique makes explicit those daydreams on which our judgment of what is important in history are, always have been, and must be based is no doubt an embarrassment; but, to those who have stomach for this sort of game, it can become the road to a wider and truer understanding.

WILLIAM N. PARKER

HISTORY AND THEORY

That economic development should bring enormous wealth and success to some men but grinding poverty and failure to others, that the unprecedented expansion of some industries should proceed simultaneously with the rapid deterioration of others, that towns should spring up overnight in one region while the people abandon their homes in another—surely all these events seem contradictory within the same nation. Yet these apparent contradictions are prominent facts about the post-Civil War era in America.[1] Clearly the facts will not speak for themselves; to understand them, we must combine facts with theory.

A theory is a logically consistent set of assumptions and implications. It provides a means of relating facts to one another, of organizing and interpreting them so that they make sense. To avoid becoming entangled

[1] In this book the expression "post-Civil War era" refers to the years 1865–1914.

in a futile attempt to describe reality in all its detail and complexity, the assumptions state only what seems especially relevant to the question, ignoring everything else. From the set of assumptions, we can logically deduce a set of implications that constitute the theory's predictions or hypotheses. In a test, the facts may or may not conform to a hypothesis. If they do, then the theory provides a means of understanding them; if they do not, then the theory's assumptions must be rejected or modified. To be of any use, a theory must have hypotheses that could conceivably be refuted by the facts, for otherwise we cannot test it. Of course, quite different theories may be consistent with certain facts. To determine which of the competing theories is the most useful, we must consider questions for which they predict differently.[2]

To use theories in interpreting history is no novelty. Indeed, any account that goes beyond mere description to a search for causes must use some theory. But typically it is implicit, and the reader must identify it by reading between the lines. Naturally this game of theoretical hide-and-seek gives rise to misunderstandings, since the theories of the author and those of his readers often fail to correspond. Moreover, when the theory is not specified, it is frequently unclear whether the question at issue is really a testable hypothesis and whether the evidence considered is appropriate. To avoid such problems, this chapter makes explicit the theoretical foundation on which the analysis of this book rests. It is hardly surprising that economists have devised the most useful theories for interpreting economic history.

MARKET ORGANIZATION

In relation to the desire for them, economic goods—both commodities and services—are always scarce. Resources being limited, it is impossible to satisfy all wants simultaneously, and people must choose among the alternatives open to them. Should more houses be built? If so, how many, and where? Who will occupy them? By what methods should they be constructed? Millions of such unavoidable choices face every society every

[2] For a lucid discussion of scientific theories in economics, see Milton Friedman, *Essays in Positive Economics* (Chicago: University of Chicago, 1953), pp. 3–43. Friedman's essay is particularly valuable for its emphasis that scientific theories cannot be judged by the "realism" of their assumptions. The most useful theory is the one that yields the most accurate predictions. For an excellent discussion of scientific theories in general, see Karl R. Popper, *The Logic of Scientific Discovery* (New York: Harper Torchbooks, 1965).

day, and the way we make the choices determines the allocation of scarce resources among alternative uses. If, for example, we commit resources to housing construction, then we necessarily forego their use elsewhere, and the most highly valued alternatives foregone constitute the true cost—what economists call the "opportunity cost"—of the housing.

Throughout the post-Civil War era in America free individuals acting within markets made most of these choices.[3] No one planned or directed the organization of economic life in any formal, overall way. Individuals themselves decided what, how much, where, when, and how to produce. Yet even though each person pursued his own designs, the overall result was not chaotic; instead, it was orderly and in many ways predictable.

Private property rights are the foundation of the market system of resource allocation. These rights permit an individual to exclude others from the use of his property and to transfer this exclusive ability to others on terms that are mutually agreeable. In a market economy, people often exchange only the rights over the use of property, not the property itself. Secure and well-defined private property rights permit individuals to transact exchanges with the expectation that agreements reached by mutual consent of the contracting parties will be binding. Without this security a market economy cannot function. Within a system of private property rights, individuals who own the means of production may sell them or use them as they see fit; similarly, people are free to dispose of their incomes as they please. Fortunately, in such a system it will usually be in the interest of individuals to act in a way that is also socially desirable, because if many people want more of a particular good, their additional expenditures for it will make its production more remunerative, enticing self-interested producers to provide more of it. These producers, in turn, will bid up the prices of resources to attract them away from their present employment and into more valuable uses.

Relative prices play a crucial role in the market system, their function

[3] The concept of a market is rather complicated. "From the point of view of a consumer, the market consists of those firms from which the consumer could buy the product; from the point of view of the producer, the market consists of those buyers to whom he could sell the product. The factors that delineate a given market depend partly on the prices that prevail, partly on the point of view being examined, and partly on such factors as distance. Other complications include the fact that the area of a market for a product is partially dependent on the nature of that product, and that we may have difficulty in defining the product exactly; in fact, the same product may have different market definitions for different buyers." See Richard G. Lipsey and Peter O. Steiner, *Economics* (New York: Harper and Row, 1966), p. 249. Resource markets, especially those for labor and loanable funds, display additional complexities.

being to summarize in a form that is immediately meaningful to consumers and producers a mass of information concerning the relative scarcity of resources, the relative efficiency of competing methods of production, and the relative urgency of different desires. Consumers tend to buy more of goods that have become relatively cheaper; workers tend to move to jobs where wage rates have become relatively higher; and producers tend to move to industries or locations where rates of return have become relatively higher. Even in the absence of conscious direction, the actions of individuals pursuing their own self-interest result in an allocation of producers, workers, and other resources that insures that the goods society wants most urgently—as expressed by freely made expenditures—will appear on the market. Similarly, because producers can increase their returns by reducing their costs, they will seek to combine their resources in the most efficient way, which benefits society by making available the most goods obtainable from the limited resources at its disposal.

The market system operates successfully only when consumers, workers, and producers perceive and respond to the signals of changing relative prices. If movements into particular industries or locations are obstructed—in other words, if competition is less than perfect—resources will be misallocated. Society then loses, because it obtains fewer goods than it could under a perfectly competitive allocation of its resources. The monopolization of markets is therefore socially undesirable. To perform well, the market system depends crucially on the free competition of consumers, workers, and producers.

The American economy in the post-Civil War era was not perfectly competitive, which is hardly surprising, since perfect competition is only a "model" that is never observed in the real world. But despite much talk about "monopolies" and "the rise of trusts," the degree to which the actual economy departed from the theoretical constructs was not great, and therefore we can still interpret the economic history of this period by applying the theory of competitive markets. Indeed, no alternative interpretation yields such an extensive array of hypotheses consistent with the facts.

THE ECONOMICS OF INFORMATION

The preceding discussion of the market system implicitly assumed that all persons possess complete information about the economy. In fact, information itself is a scarce good. It is therefore not free, and individuals must economize in their search for it; everyone must necessarily remain ignorant to some extent. Recognizing the economic basis of ignorance, however, permits us to explain a wide range of historical events for which the simple theory of competitive markets cannot account and at the same time to explain the emergence and growth of a variety of businesses whose main purpose is the creation or dissemination of information.

An example will help to present the basic ideas of the economics of information. Consider a man seeking a job. Other things being the same, he prefers the job with the highest wage rate; but his problem is to find it. Wages differ somewhat from place to place, and changes occur from time to time. (Wage dispersion exists because it typically does not pay an employer to find out exactly what wage rate each of his competitors pays for each grade of labor.) Suppose the job seeker inquires at the nearest factory and finds that he could obtain a job there at $2.00 per hour. Would it pay to look any further? By searching for alternative jobs he incurs costs in two ways: first, he loses the wages he could be earning had he accepted the first job; second, he must sacrifice leisure and incur direct costs in transporting himself about in search of alternatives. But potential gains exist, too. He may discover that the next factory pays $2.25 per hour. If he believes that wages in the neighborhood typically vary widely, he will probably continue his search. Also, if many factories are located nearby, he will be more likely to continue the search than if he had to go to the next town to find another opportunity. He will arrive at a decision by balancing the expected gains from seeking additional information against the expected costs of acquiring it. If expected costs exceed expected gains he will stop searching and seize on the best opportunity found so far; if the converse is true he will continue searching.

If many workers are seeking jobs, a new business is likely to appear. Someone will probably establish an employment agency, keeping informed of job openings, wage rates, working conditions, and skill requirements, and providing this information to job seekers for a price. Since this agency can probably collect information more effectively than the average worker because of its established contacts and accumulated experience, and because once collected the information can be provided to additional persons at very small cost, the employment agency represents a means of greatly enhancing the efficiency of the labor market. Workers need not continue searching for information from place to place. By eliminating repetitious inquiries, the employment agency greatly reduces the quantity of resources used in search activities. The average length of time each worker is unemployed while seeking a new job will probably fall. Employers also gain, because they can now obtain qualified new employees more readily by advertising with the agency. Workers gain, employers gain, and the owner of the employment agency obtains an income that compensates him for his efforts.

We can easily generalize this example. Whether the question is the worker's search for the highest-paying job, the consumer's search for the lowest-priced, highest-quality products, or the businessman's search for the most remunerative investment opportunities, the same principles apply. In general, the greater the values involved, the greater are the potential gains, and therefore the greater is the amount of search. On the other hand, the larger the market geographically or the higher the costs of transportation and communication, the greater are the costs of search, and therefore the amount of search will be correspondingly reduced. However, the larger the market, not only geographically but also in terms of dollar volume and the number of traders, the more likely information-supplying businesses such as trade journals or brokers are to appear. (We say only "more likely" because discovering the opportunities for obtaining an income by supplying information is also a costly endeavor, and it would not pay anyone to find them all.) In this way business organization adapts to the changing size and demand patterns of the market. By pursuing gains from the provision of information, businessmen—without necessarily knowing or caring about the implications of their efforts—help the whole market system to operate more efficiently.

INVESTMENT AND ECONOMIC GROWTH

In the long run men can consume no more than they produce. The maximum possible output of goods depends on the number of available workers and the size of the capital stock, the produced means of production. Of course, if the labor force grows, more can be produced; and if the capital stock grows proportionately with the labor force, still more can be produced. But even then, we cannot expect the amount of output per worker to increase much. In a larger economy men can specialize to a greater degree, and this specialization can raise the average output per worker. It is difficult, however, to imagine such improvements continuing for long *solely* as a result of the increasing scale of the economy.

Economic growth means a continuing increase in output per person sustained over the long run, at least over several decades. Such a productivity increase permits, on the average, rising levels of material well-being. Economic growth does not just happen, however. Its gains are the product of deliberate human efforts.

Economic growth results from the accumulation of capital through a continuing series of investments. An increase in the amount of capital the average worker has to assist him in production enables him to produce more output. The relevant stock of capital embraces not only buildings, machinery, equipment, inventories, and improved land, but also the acquired health and skills of the labor force; most important of all, it includes the technology, the body of knowledge relating inputs of resources to outputs of goods.[4] It is useful, then, to distinguish at least three kinds of capital—material, human, and intellectual. In the long run it is impossible to build up one part of the capital stock without also building up the others. The Commissioner of Patents in 1900 clearly recognized this interdependence: "To employ these devices [American inventions] to the best advantage requires the intelligence of the American workmen, and the result is due to the combination of witty inventions and thinking men. Witless men behind witty machines would be of no use."[5] Understanding these interdependencies is at the heart of understanding the process of economic growth, but unfortunately scholars have devoted little attention to them. To build factories is commonly recognized as an investment, but to obtain education, to purchase improved health, to seek new useful knowledge—these too are investments. And the rate of return on investment in a particular kind of capital depends not only on the size of the existing stock but also on the available stocks of complementary kinds of capital.

Information flows are intimately involved in these interdependent investments. The accumulation of intellectual capital, sometimes called technological progress, is simply the augmentation of the stock of useful information about production processes. Investments in the improvement of health often rely on new knowledge of public hygiene and disease or on the wider application of old knowledge. And education, of course, is nothing more than the dissemination of information. Moreover, even material capital accumulation does not stand completely outside this conceptual framework, for new ideas are often useful only when embodied in new capital goods. Investment in material capital then becomes the vehicle for the implementation of technological advance. In an important sense, the economics of rising productivity and the economics of information are inseparable.

Investors generally undertake a project only when the expected returns exceed those obtainable from employing the available resources in their best alternative use. No one would quarrel with this proposition as applied to investments in material capital, but because we have not traditionally considered invention and education as investments, it may be useful to see some examples.

[4] To some extent the technology can be augmented without a commitment of resources to that purpose, through learning from experience. This kind of technological progress is considered below, pp. 103–105.

[5] U. S. Patent Office [C. H. Duell], *Annual Report of the Commissioner of Patents for 1900* (Washington: Government Printing Office, 1901), p. ix.

Consider a hypothetical individual who is contemplating the development and production of a new tool, such as a machine for making nails. Before committing himself to such a project, the inventor will have to form several expectations. First, he needs to know the probable costs of developing and producing such a machine. These costs include not only the money outlays he must make but also the value of the best alternative use of his time and talent he foregoes by working on the project, both items together comprising his full "opportunity cost." Second, he must estimate, for each year in which his machine will be purchased, the number he can sell at the price he will charge, which tells him the stream of revenues he can expect from future sales. By subtracting the probable costs of production from these yearly revenues, he finds the expected net revenue stream. He can then calculate the present value of the future net revenues.[6] If the present value of the expected net revenue stream exceeds the development costs, the inventor considers the project worth while and undertakes it. If at one time the project is not worth while but later becomes so, it is because the development cost or the rate of return on the best alternative opportunity has fallen, or because the expected net revenue stream has increased. If, for example, the construction industry grows and the demand for nails increases, then the market for nail-making machinery will be enlarged, and this augmentation of the expected net revenue stream may make the project worth while.

Suppose the inventor undertakes to develop and sell his machine but finds that others then imitate it and "rob" him of sales. Such copying may well turn his expected gains into actual losses. If, however, some legal institution—a patent system—insures that he can capture sufficient gains from his idea, the risk of such "robbery" is reduced; he will therefore be more likely to undertake the project. The patent grant gives the inventor a temporary monopoly over the use of his idea in exchange for its public disclosure. In general, we suppose that monopolies obstruct economic growth, but here the gains that accrue from technological progress can

[6] The calculation of the present value is necessary because receipts at different points in time are not directly comparable. A dollar receivable next year is worth less than a dollar receivable today because today's dollar can be used to produce earnings —for example, by lending it at interest—or because it can be used for immediate consumption, but one has no command over the dollar receivable next year. Immediate availability commands a positive price, the rate of interest. If receipts $R(1)$, $R(2)$, . . . , $R(n)$ are expected to be receivable after 1, 2, . . . , n years, the present value of the revenue stream is given by the formula:

$$\text{Present value} = \frac{R(1)}{(1+i)} + \frac{R(2)}{(1+i)^2} + \ldots + \frac{R(n)}{(1+i)^n}$$

where i is the rate of return on one's best alternative investment. See Armen A. Alchian and William R. Allen, *University Economics*, 2d ed. (Belmont, Calif.: Wadsworth, 1967), pp. 199–209.

more than compensate for the temporary withholding of information. While the inventor himself receives the encouragement of capturable gains, the overall result can be a gain for society. As the Commissioner of Patents saw very clearly in 1891, "The patent law does not exist for the benefit of inventors. It exists for the benefit of the public."[7]

Our hypothetical case suggests some general propositions. Whether an invention will be produced depends on the relation between two variables: the expected revenues it will generate, and the expected costs of developing it. Expected revenues are often closely related to the growth of the market—that is, to the expansion of population or income per capita and to the reduction of transportation costs. Expected development costs may decline with the discovery of new scientific knowledge or with the appearance of related inventions. But no matter how promising an invention may appear in a social sense, few inventors will undertake a project unless they expect to reap sufficient gains from their ideas. Private property rights must be defined and enforced for intellectual property as well as for material property if much technological progress is to occur in a market economy.

Consider now a young man contemplating the choice of an occupation in the 1840's. His interests incline him toward work in designing machinery, toward what we now call mechanical engineering. He soon recognizes, however, that it will not be in his best interests to undertake the several years of specialized education necessary to prepare for such work, because very few jobs of this sort are available. Most firms are small and use little machinery; what they do use they generally design, install, and service themselves as the need arises. The demand for machinery is too small to support a machinery industry where mechanical engineers would be demanded in greater numbers. The young man may well decide to become a carpenter, which requires a shorter and less expensive period of training and offers abundant opportunities for employment.

If we shift our attention forward to the 1870's and consider the occupation selected by the carpenter's son, who has interests like his father's, the choice of occupation may well be different. By this time there are many more firms, each one on the average using more machinery. Consequently the demand for machinery is substantially larger, and a separate

[7] U. S. Patent Office [W. E. Simonds], *Annual Report of the Commissioner of Patents for 1891* (Washington: Government Printing Office, 1892), p. v. Whether the benefits of the American patent system actually have outweighed its costs is a hotly debated question. It is really a question of fact, but the facts in this case are particularly difficult to determine, for both conceptual and empirical reasons. For an excellent discussion of this complex problem, see Fritz Machlup, "Patents," in *International Encyclopedia of the Social Sciences* (New York: Macmillan, 1968).

industry supplying machinery is beginning to emerge. As a result the demand for mechanical engineers is greater, and it may now pay to undertake the education necessary to prepare for this occupation. The son becomes a mechanical engineer. He is more skilled than his father, and his skills are reflected in his higher real earnings.

This example can be generalized to explain why the entire labor force becomes more skilled in a growing economy. The larger the market, the greater is the number of highly skilled, specialized jobs that the market will support. The more potential jobs, the greater is the incentive for workers to invest in becoming skilled specialists. In principle, the person considering an investment in acquiring skills would calculate the present value of the expected net revenue stream associated with having such skills and compare that with the opportunity cost of the training. As in the case of other economic decisions, it need not be true that individuals actually make such elaborate calculations; even though they reach their decisions by considering their alternatives only in a rough-and-ready fashion, still they generally act *as if* they had performed such calculations. And even if initial decisions were randomly made, only the "correct" ones would be rewarded in the market. Observation of such accidental successes would then encourage subsequent decision makers to move in the most rewarding direction.[8]

TRANSFORMATION

As incomes rise, the demand for some goods grows even more rapidly, while the demand for other goods hardly increases at all. The amount spent on food, for example, grows relatively slower than incomes, and therefore consumers spend a progressively smaller proportion of their incomes on food. For other goods, like personal transportation or recreation, expenditures grow faster than income, and such goods come to occupy a larger part of consumers' budgets. Because of such changing demand patterns, relative prices are altered as incomes grow, and the rate of return on the production of some goods is enhanced while that of other goods deteriorates. These changes induce wealth-seeking businessmen to expand the production of goods for which the demand is growing most rapidly, and in the process they bid up the prices of resources to attract them into the expanding industries. The upshot of these actions

[8] Armen A. Alchian, "Uncertainty, Evolution, and Economic Theory," *Journal of Political Economy*, LX (June 1950); and Milton Friedman, *Essays in Positive Economics*, pp. 16–23.

is a reallocation of resources among industries and a change in the composition of the economy's total output. In this way resources have shifted out of agriculture and into manufacturing, transportation, and services during the past century and a half.

Similar reallocations of resources occur because productivity—output per unit of input—typically grows at different rates among industries, because, for example, the pace of technological progress is greater in some industries than in others. Gains in productivity reduce the costs of production, which increases the rate of return to entrepreneurs. Greater returns induce other producers to enter the industry, and this entry—along with the expansion of existing producers—expands supply, driving prices down and attracting more buyers. Eventually, excessive entrepreneurial returns are eliminated as prices fall, and new entry into the industry ceases; but in the process a redistribution of output and resources among industries occurs. For example, in steel making, where productivity advanced very rapidly during the post-Civil War era, output also expanded more rapidly than in most other industries, and the steel industry grew from an "infant" into one of the nation's largest.

Finally, because of discovery, depletion, accumulation, or migration, changes occur over time in the resources—both human and nonhuman—available in particular places. These changes in resource endowment affect the rates of return on different economic activities, inducing a reallocation of enterprises among regions. When Ohio was first settled, for example, its economic activities were primarily agricultural, but by 1914 the state was, by comparison with other states, heavily engaged in manufacturing. This change occurred because skilled workers migrated to Ohio and because entrepreneurs accumulated much material capital there during the nineteenth century. With its resource endowment in 1914 the state was best suited for nonagricultural activities, and farming had largely shifted to states farther west, where the resource endowment was relatively favorable to agriculture.

In sum, we can identify at least three important concomitants of economic growth: changing patterns of demand; differing rates of productivity gain among industries; and changing resource endowments among regions. Among the important transformations that these forces produce in a market economy are: changes in the composition of the economy's total output; changes in the distribution of productive resources, including workers, among industries; and regional shifts in production and employment. (Another important aspect of transformation, urbanization, is discussed in some detail in Chapter III.)

Not everyone welcomes these changes, and some people actively resist them. New ideas, new skills, and new machinery add to the economy's average productivity, but they also give rise to a different distribution of the total product. Those committed to old skills or obsolete machinery, employed in declining industries, or located in areas where important natural resources are exhausted, often suffer. Although changes in the relative income and wealth of different groups are inherent in the process of economic growth, those who suffer the relative (and sometimes absolute) losses have rarely perceived the true source of their misfortune. Often they have ascribed responsibility for their hardship to the successful groups; typically they have sought government intervention to protect them from the vagaries of the market. Of course, people need not be misinformed to react in these ways. Much of what is nowadays described as the "farm problem," for example, is nothing more than an attempt to resist the transformation of agriculture, to maintain a larger amount of resources in farming than can be supported there without assistance from the government. Many modern farmers surely understand their dilemma; their political actions furnish a good example of a well-informed effort to obstruct the economy's transformation. To the extent that people fail to adjust to the economy's transformed structure, economic growth is retarded. Transformation is not only a consequence of growth; it is a condition for further growth. However, for those who must make the adjustments, this transformation is often a painful and costly process, and the economic historian's inability to measure many of these costs makes them no less real. David A. Wells summarized the issue clearly in 1889 when he said that "pending the interval or necessary period for adjustment, the problem of what to do to prevent a mass of adults, whose previous education has not qualified them for taking advantage of the new opportunities which material progress offers to them, from sinking into wretchedness and perhaps permanent poverty, is a serious one, and one not easy to answer."[9] Ultimately, of course, no one offered an "answer"; people simply struggled as best they could, sometimes failing utterly. The market system could be efficient to the point of ruthlessness. Inevitably, transformation affected not only economic welfare but political power and social status as well; new attitudes and values appeared in the process. Measuring the growth of per capita income is only a very crude way of indicating a population's changing well-being, but clearly welfare in a more all-embracing sense is inextricably tied to economic growth and transformation.

[9] David A. Wells, *Recent Economic Changes* (New York: Appleton, 1889), p. 437.

II

ECONOMIC GROWTH AND TRANSFORMATION

> The American at home, spinning along with his country, can obtain little idea of the amazing rate at which she is moving in comparison with other parts of the world. It is only when he sits down and studies statistics that he becomes almost dizzy at discovering the velocity with which she is rushing on. . . . It is probable that in many future decades the citizen is to look back upon this as the golden age of the Republic and long for a return of its conditions.
>
> ANDREW CARNEGIE

OUTPUT AND PRICE TRENDS

In the 1840's and 1850's, and perhaps even earlier, output per capita increased quite rapidly, but the Civil War brought economic progress to a halt. In fact, standards of living fell during the war for most people on both sides. This decline is hardly surprising, for war always diverts resources from productive to destructive uses, and the Civil War was America's most devastating experience. More than 600,000 men—over 5 percent of the labor force—most of them young adults, died in the conflict. In the South physical destruction was widespread. To make matters worse, the landless emancipation of the slaves, decreed by President Lincoln and later ratified by constitutional amendment, caused organizational chaos in the economic life of the South that had permanently harmful consequences. But not until the political issues had been

TABLE 2.1

REAL GROSS NATIONAL PRODUCT PER CAPITA AND IMPLICIT PRICE INDEX

Period	Annual Average GNP per Capita (1860 dollars) (1)	Implicit Price Index (2)
1869–1878	147	123
1874–1883	172	115
1879–1888	193	106
1884–1893	208	97
1889–1898	213	92
1894–1903	234	94
1899–1908	268	103

SOURCE. Col. 1: calculated from GNP data in Robert E. Gallman, "Gross National Product in the United States, 1834–1909," in National Bureau of Economic Research, Conference on Research in Income and Wealth, *Output, Employment, and Productivity in the United States after 1800* (New York: Columbia University, 1966), p. 30 and population data in U. S. Bureau of the Census, *Long Term Economic Growth, 1860–1965* (Washington: Government Printing Office, 1966), p. 182. Col. 2: Gallman, *loc. cit.*

settled on the battlefield were Americans ready to return to the business of economic progress.

The economy grew spectacularly in the half century following the war. Real GNP per capita advanced at an average rate of 2 percent per year, and on the eve of World War I it stood at about three times the 1865 level (Table 2.1).[1] Total output expanded even more astoundingly: real GNP grew at an average rate of more than 4 percent per year, increasing about eightfold over the period. Never before had such rapid

[1] Gross national product, usually abbreviated GNP, is defined as the value at market prices of all final goods produced in a year. It is the most common measure of an economy's total output. Notice that we count only *final* commodities and services. For example, suppose a farmer sells wheat to a miller, who makes it into flour for sale to a baker, who makes it into bread for sale to final consumers. Only the bread is a final good; the wheat and the flour are *intermediate* goods. By accounting convention, we consider durable capital goods and additions to inventories final, even though their sole purpose is to enlarge the capacity to produce, and therefore they are intermediate in an important sense. By speaking of a change in *real* GNP we refer to a comparison of two collections of goods valued at the same prices. Since prices typically change over time, we can make reliable statements about growth or decline of output only by weighting goods with constant prices. See Armen A. Alchian and William R. Allen, *University Economics*, 2d ed. (Belmont, Calif.: Wadsworth, 1967), pp. 513–16.

growth continued for so long. Of course, growth did not occur in a perfectly smooth, regular fashion. Business fluctuations punctuated the whole era, particularly severe depressions occurring in the mid-1870's and the mid-1890's. As always in an unregulated market economy, growth proceeded in fits and starts.

After the war, despite brief inflations during the expansion phases of business fluctuations, the trend of the overall price level was downward until 1897. A reversal then occurred, and a generally rising price level characterized the two decades before America's entry into World War I (Table 2.1). Changes in the stock of money and in total real output underlay these long phases of deflation and inflation.[2]

We can clarify these relations by considering the equation $P = \frac{MV}{Y}$ where P is the overall price level, M is the money stock in dollars, V is the average number of times that a dollar is spent for currently produced final goods each year, and Y is the quantity of real output. The equation merely states that the price level is, by definition, a ratio of money expenditure (MV) to real quantity purchased (Y). We can transform this definition into a theory of the price level by assuming that over the long run—say, over several decades—V is approximately constant, which is equivalent to assuming that the amount of money the public wishes to hold is a constant fraction of its money income. Changes in the price level, then, depend on changes in the money stock and in real output. If Y increases faster than M, prices will tend to fall because the quantity of goods grows faster than aggregate expenditures, and the total output can be sold only if its average price is reduced. Conversely, when M increases faster than Y, prices will tend to rise.

During the three decades of deflation before 1897, the money stock —including gold and silver coins, bank notes and deposits, and various obligations of the federal government—increased, but not as fast as real output increased. Immediately after the war, the federal government helped to slow monetary growth by reducing the quantity of its fiat money, the famous "greenbacks," as a step toward reestablishing the currency/gold exchange rate at its prewar level. The government steadfastly resisted the demands of the Greenback Labor Party and others for a large issue of new fiat currency. After 1874, when its free market price fell below its mint price, silver could have pushed the money stock up, but the law provided for only a limited coinage of this metal, and its

[2] The following analysis of price trends is highly simplified. For a detailed account, see Milton Friedman and Anna J. Schwartz, *A Monetary History of the United States, 1867–1960* (Princeton, N. J.: Princeton University, 1963), pp. 15–188.

actual contribution to monetary growth was slight. Under the *de facto* gold standard after 1878, the stock of money could not vary independently of the gold stock, for besides serving directly as a medium of exchange, gold provided the convertibility reserves on which the quantity of bank notes and deposits depended. Therefore, the growth of the entire money stock was tied to production of the yellow metal, and for 30 years gold production simply did not keep pace with the outpouring of commodities and services. Falling prices were the consequence. After 1897, discoveries of gold in the Yukon, South Africa, and elsewhere, combined with newly devised, more efficient techniques of mining and refining, rapidly expanded the supply of gold and pushed the money stock up faster than real output. The price level rose. Notably, rapid economic growth occurred both before and after 1897; neither a falling nor a rising general price level was uniquely associated with economic growth.

POPULATION GROWTH

Growing at an average rate of over 2 percent per year, the population of the United States almost trebled between 1865 and 1915 (Table 2.2). But a tendency toward slower growth marked the period; the annual

TABLE 2.2

POPULATION AND LABOR FORCE

Year	Population (Millions) (1)	Labor Force (Millions) (2)
1865	36	12
1870	40	13
1880	50	17
1890	60	23
1900	76	29
1910	92	37
1915	101	40

SOURCE. Col. 1: U. S. Bureau of the Census, *Historical Statistics of the United States, Colonial Times to 1957* (Washington: Government Printing Office, 1960), p. 7. Col. 2: figures for 1870–1910 from Stanley Lebergott, "Labor Force and Employment, 1800–1960," in National Bureau of Economic Research, Conference on Research in Income and Wealth, *Output, Employment, and Productivity in the United States after 1800* (New York: Columbia University, 1966), p. 118; figures for 1865 and 1915 obtained by extrapolation from Lebergott's data.

rate of growth fell from about 2.3 percent during the early years (1865–80) to about 1.9 percent at the end of the period (1900–15). The country's population grew because births exceeded deaths and because the number of immigrants exceeded the number of emigrants. Despite unprecedented immigration, natural increase contributed far more to the growth of the population. In the 1870's the birth rate was probably more than 40 per thousand of population, while the death rate was in the neighborhood of 23; therefore, the rate of natural increase was at least 17 per thousand. Both birth and death rates declined subsequently, and the gap between them became somewhat narrower. Just before World War I the birth rate had fallen below 30, the death rate to about 15, and hence the rate of natural increase to less than 15.

A decline in the birth rate has characterized every nation that has experienced economic growth, and it is closely related to the transformation that accompanies growth. In particular, the migration from the countryside to the cities led to a decline in the desired family size, and hence to a reduction in the number of births per family. On the farm large families furnished hands that, given the nature and organization of work there, could be set to useful tasks at an early age. But in the city the costs of rearing and educating children were greater, while their economic usefulness was smaller. There women found greater opportunities for working outside the home, and hence child rearing involved higher foregone incomes. An incentive therefore arose for limiting the number of children. Other influences also helped to reduce the birth rate. For example, with lower child mortality, a family required fewer births to achieve the desired number of surviving children. But declining fertility probably owed more to urbanization than to any other single cause. Since urbanization was a consequence of economic growth, an ultimate source of retardation in the rate of population growth was economic growth itself.[3]

A falling death rate resulted from better public health practices and from the improved standards of living that accompanied rising levels of output per capita. Improvements in sanitation, water supply, sewerage, nutrition, and housing all helped to reduce the incidence of infectious diseases like tuberculosis and typhoid. Advances in medical practice had

[3] This brief discussion necessarily omits many aspects of the secular decline in fertility. For detailed analysis and description, see Gary S. Becker, "An Economic Analysis of Fertility," in National Bureau of Economic Research, *Demographic and Economic Change in Developed Countries* (Princeton, N. J.: Princeton University, 1960), pp. 209–31, and comments by James S. Duesenberry and Bernard Okun, pp. 231–40; and E. A. Wrigley, *Population and History* (New York: McGraw-Hill, 1969), especially pp. 217–24.

little or no impact on the death rate. Again, as in the case of the declining birth rate, economic growth itself was a principal source of the change. (Later in this chapter and in Chapter III we discuss health improvements in more detail.)

The greatest volume of immigration in recorded history augmented the natural increase of the population. After the Civil War the rate of alien arrivals reached an unprecedented high, and the trend continued upward until the First World War reduced the inflow to a trickle. In the 1920's the imposition of legal quotas finally closed the doors on the age of massive, unrestricted immigration. Before the 1890's the so-called "old" immigration predominated, having its sources primarily in the United Kingdom, Germany, and the Scandinavian countries. Beginning in the 1890's and extending until the war, the so-called "new" immigration accounted for the greater part of the influx. These people came mainly from southern and eastern Europe, with Italy supplying the most, followed closely by Austria-Hungary and Russia. Throughout the post-Civil War era immigration followed a rough correspondence with fluctuations of prosperity and depression in the United States, all the great surges of immigration occurring during periods of American prosperity (Figure 2.1). The reduced employment opportunities that accompanied the business depressions of 1873–1878, 1882–1885, 1893–1897, and 1908 are mirrored in the troughs of the net immigration cycle that correspond to those dates. The push of hard times in the countries of origin undoubtedly played a part also, especially in determining what parts of Europe would contribute most heavily, but the timing of the migrations seems to have been influenced more decisively by the pull of prosperous

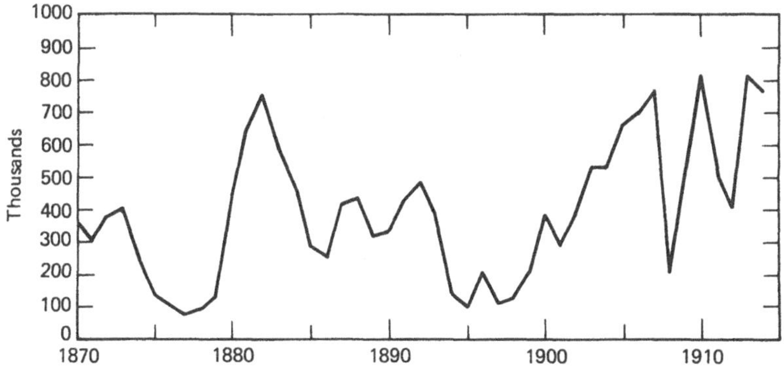

Figure 2.1 Arrivals minus departures, all alien passengers. *Source:* Simon Kuznets and Ernest Rubin, *Immigration and the Foreign Born* (New York: National Bureau of Economic Research, 1954), p. 95.

conditions in the United States. In total, more than 28 million immigrants entered between 1865 and 1915. Perhaps as many as a third eventually returned to Europe, putting net immigration in the neighborhood of 20 million persons. Immigrants provided a large part of the additions to the population in some decades. At the peaks, in the 1880's and 1900's, they accounted for about a fifth of the increase in population. Being heavily concentrated in the young adult ages, they constituted an even larger proportion of the total additions to the labor force, at times as much as 30 percent.

A rapidly growing population had major economic consequences. Most importantly, it provided a growing labor force (Table 2.2). In fact, the labor force grew even more rapidly than the population, because the immigrants augmented the working-aged population proportionately more than the dependent-aged population and because as the birth rate fell the ratio of adults (workers) to children increased. Population growth also expanded the number of consumers, broadening markets and permitting a greater degree of specialization. A rapidly growing population buoyed up investors' confidence in future market conditions, encouraging them to bear risks in expanding the capital stock. In comparison with Europe, the United States was an economy of labor scarcity and low population density. In such a setting, population growth never operated as a drag on economic growth but rather encouraged the capital accumulation that gave rise to economic progress.

THE SOURCES OF GREATER PRODUCTIVITY

Our understanding of economic growth would be greatly advanced if we could say just how much each source of growth—material capital formation, education, technological progress, and so forth—contributed toward increasing output. In recent years economists have developed several techniques for attributing economic growth to its various sources. Unfortunately, however, it is impossible to provide a very detailed breakdown, and the calculations are subject to errors of unknown magnitude because the available data do not correspond very well with the theoretical concepts and because the data are not very accurate anyhow. Still, such calculations may reveal relative orders of magnitude in a broad way. The figures presented below are based on calculations shown in the Appendix, which some readers may wish to examine before reading any further.[4]

[4] The problems surrounding these calculations are both conceptual and empirical. For an introduction to the literature on productivity measurement, see Solomon

We can partition the rise in total GNP during the 1869–1914 period roughly as follows: the increase in the number of man-hours worked accounts for about four tenths; the expansion of the material capital stock, including land, explains about three tenths; and all other sources account for the remaining three tenths. Partitioning the growth of output *per man-hour,* we find that the increase in the ratio of material capital to labor explains over one fourth, and all other sources account for almost three fourths. Crude as these conclusions may be, they are nevertheless of great significance, for they indicate that economic growth—a sustained increase in output per capita—cannot, as economists believed for a long time, be attributed mainly to material capital accumulation. We must not, of course, dismiss material capital accumulation as unimportant; after all, it did account for over one fourth of the increase in output per man-hour. Furthermore, we know that technological advances were often realizable only in conjunction with investment in material capital. Still, to explain economic growth, we must devote the lion's share of our attention to the accumulation of human and intellectual capital.

Material Capital Accumulation

The nineteenth century saw great expansions in the territory of the United States, which not only added to the country's arable acreage but also brought land of superior quality into use. Besides farming land, the acquisitions contained vast amounts of other resources, including minerals, timber, and grass. The 1840's saw a flurry of territorial expansion: Texas was annexed in 1845; claims to the Oregon country were settled with Great Britain in 1846; and the Mexican Cession was acquired as the spoils of war in 1848. These lands added almost 70 percent to the national domain, and as late as 1865 all of them were sparsely populated, some of them virtually uninhabited.

The thrust of the population movement was inexorably westward. By 1865 the frontier—defined as an area of at least two but less than six persons per square mile, cities of 8000 or more not being considered—extended into Minnesota, Kansas, Nebraska, and Texas, and the states

Fabricant, "Productivity," in *International Encyclopedia of the Social Sciences* (New York: Macmillan, 1968). The most sophisticated contribution to this literature is Dale Jorgenson and Zvi Griliches, "The Explanation of Productivity Change," *Review of Economic Studies,* XXXIV (July 1967). But see also the important criticisms of the Jorgenson-Griliches paper by Edward F. Denison, "Some Major Issues in Productivity Analysis," *Survey of Current Business,* IL (May 1969), Pt. II. The whole field is lucidly surveyed by M. Ishaq Nadiri, "Some Approaches to the Theory and Measurement of Total Factor Productivity: A Survey," *Journal of Economic Literature,* VIII (Dec. 1970).

in the first tier west of the Mississippi were fast filling up. After the Civil War the population flooded over the trans-Mississippi prairies and the Great Plains, and the Pacific Coast states attracted hordes of migrants. The Superintendent of the Census of 1890 declared: "Up to and including 1880 the country had a frontier of settlement, but at present the unsettled area has been so broken into by isolated bodies of settlement that there can hardly be said to be a frontier line." In 1893 the historian Frederick Jackson Turner further dramatized the "closing of the frontier," and many subsequent accounts of westward expansion have placed great emphasis on this event and the date of its occurrence. Actually, the announcement was premature. The hard times of the 1890's drove both farmers and townspeople eastward, and in 1900 the frontier line miraculously reappeared (without comment) in the census maps. But its days were numbered. In 1910 the maps of settlement showed that no clear cutting edge remained of the frontier, and pockets of population dotted the area between the 100th meridian and the Pacific Coast. Thousands of words cannot compete effectively with a few maps on this subject, so the reader is referred to Figures 2.2–2.6.

It is difficult nowadays to comprehend the importance of land in the nineteenth century. Perhaps a fruitful approach is to consider how nineteenth-century economists viewed its place in the economy. The great English economist David Ricardo and his followers, among whom the influential American writer Henry George may be counted, explained that land operates as a drag on economic growth, for there is only a fixed amount of it. As poorer quality land is put into production to provide for a growing population, the higher quality land commands larger rents. And as the limit of available land is reached, the only means of expanding food production is by cultivating the land more intensively. But here we encounter the specter of diminishing returns: the addition to output obtained by successive applications of labor and material capital to a fixed amount of land tends to become progressively smaller. The real returns to labor and capital decline; both workers and capitalists are eventually impoverished, while useless landlords grow rich, and the economy ultimately arrives at a "stationary state," with a stable but mostly destitute population. Small wonder that some contemporaries called economics the "dismal science"!

In the United States the seemingly limitless availability of cheap land banished the specter of diminishing returns. In the overly optimistic words of Thomas Jefferson, there was "room enough for our descendants to the thousandth and thousandth generation." Typically the lack of transportation making it economically accessible, not a scarcity of land itself, constrained the growth of farm production. After the Civil War,

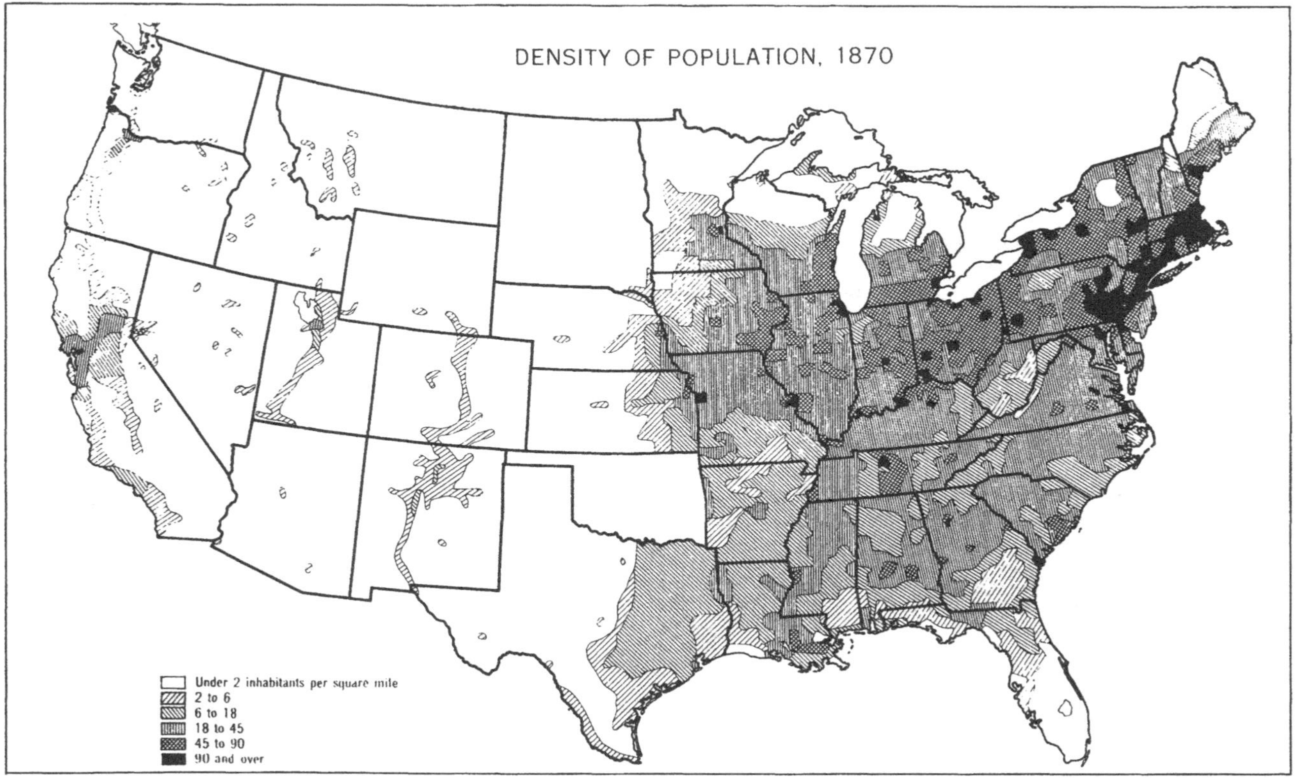

Figure 2.2 Spatial distribution of population, 1870. *Source:* C. O. Paullin, *Atlas of the Historical Geography of the United States* (Washington: Carnegie Institution, 1932), plate 77c.

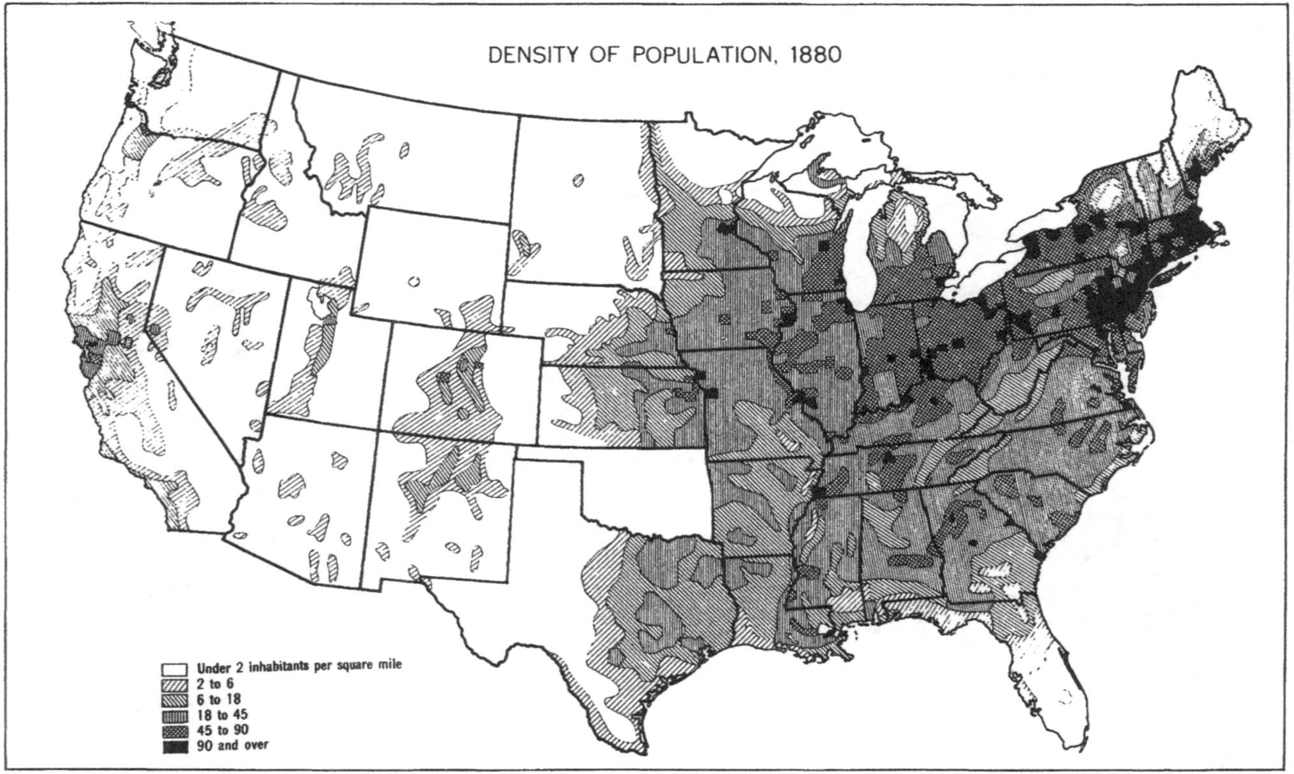

Figure 2.3 Spatial distribution of population, 1880. *Source:* C. O. Paullin, *Atlas of the Historical Geography of the United States* (Washington: Carnegie Institution, 1932), plate 78a.

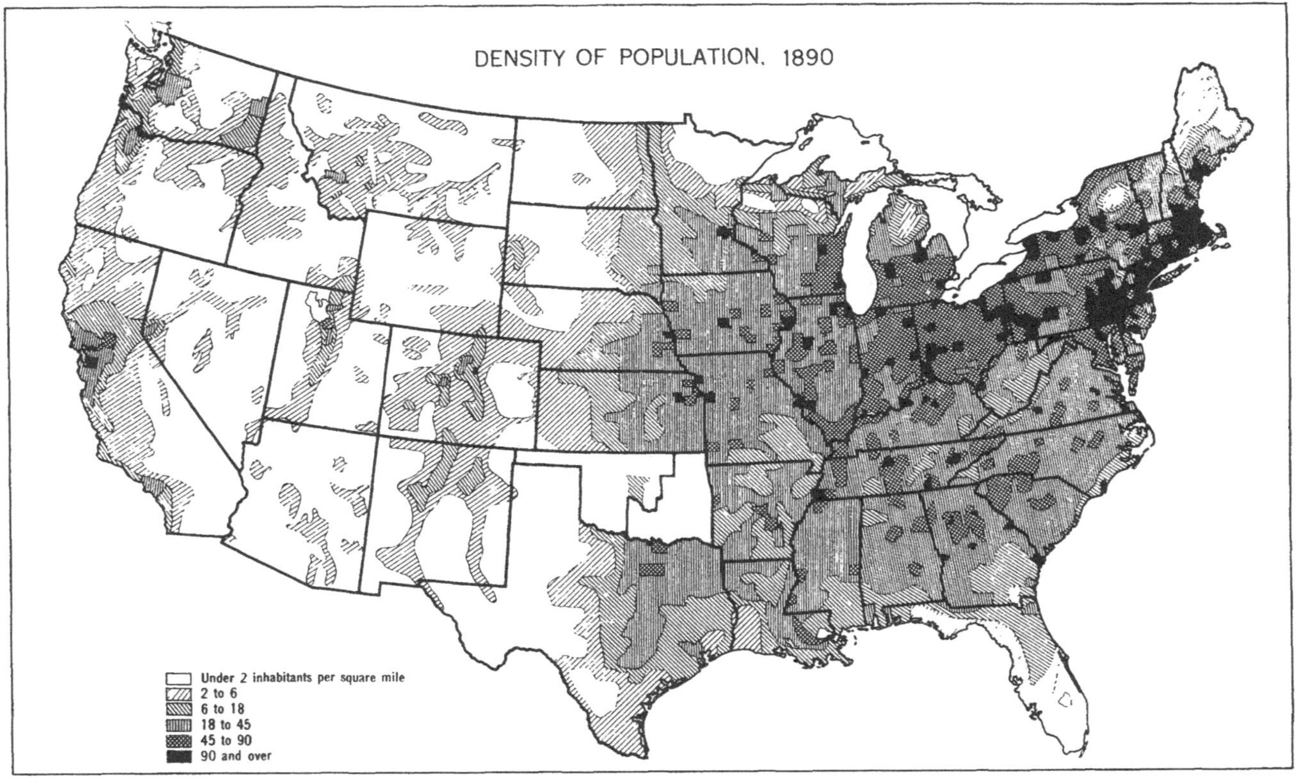

Figure 2.4 Spatial distribution of population, 1890. *Source:* C. O. Paullin, *Atlas of the Historical Geography of the United States* (Washington: Carnegie Institution, 1932), plate 78b.

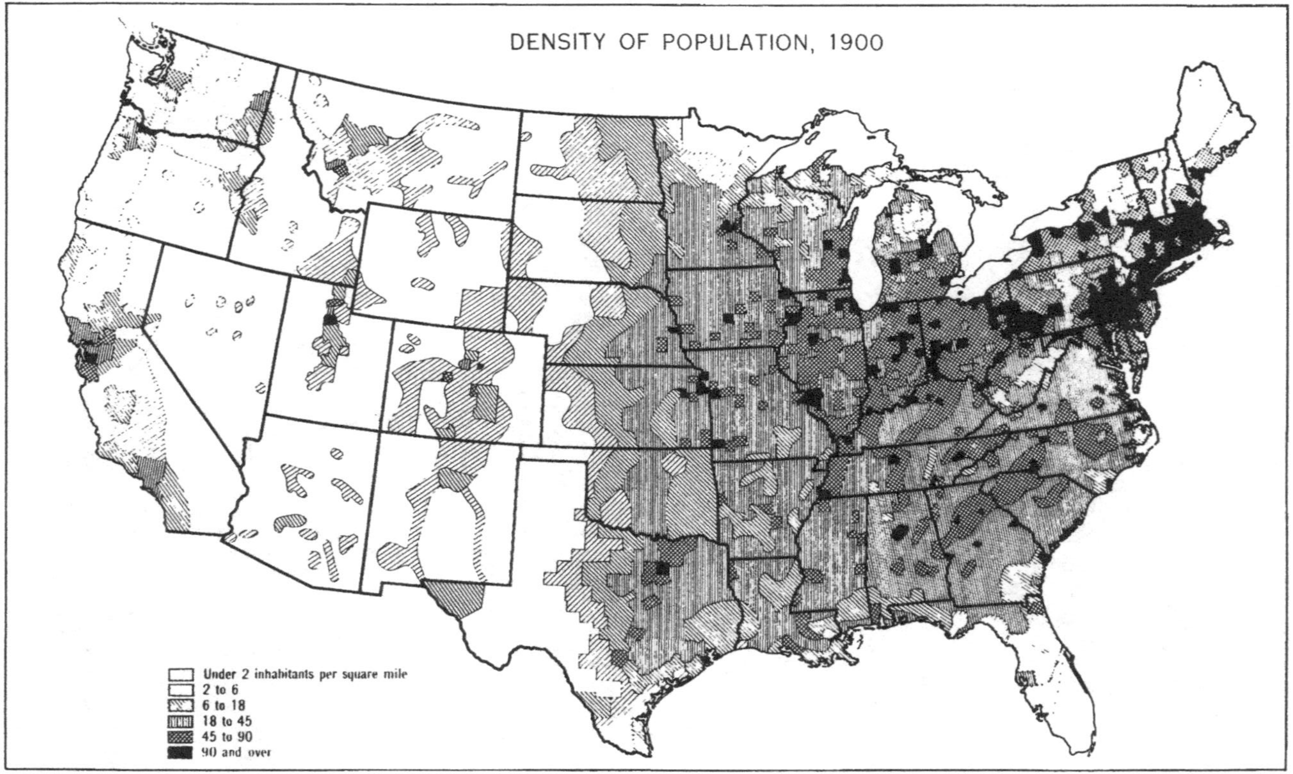

Figure 2.5 Spatial distribution of population, 1900. *Source:* C. O. Paullin, *Atlas of the Historical Geography of the United States* (Washington: Carnegie Institution, 1932), plate 79a.

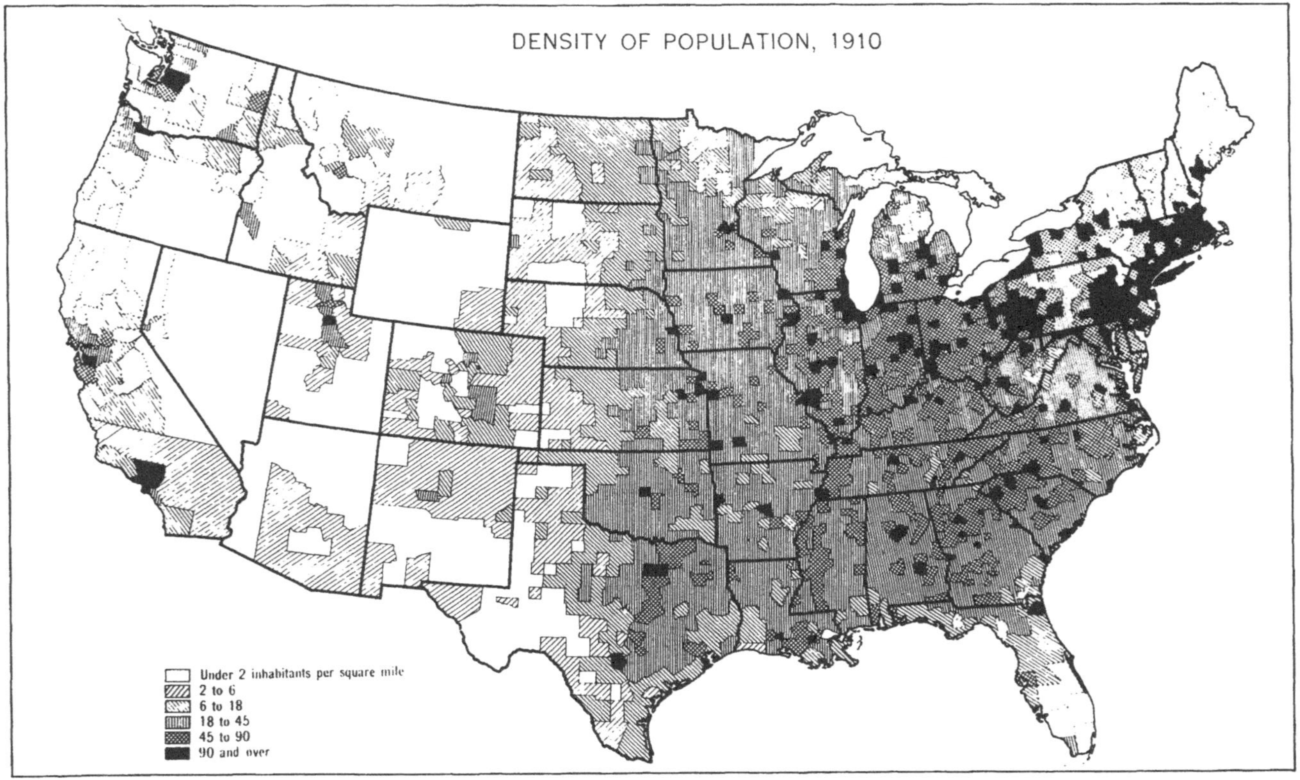

Figure 2.6 Spatial distribution of population, 1910. *Source:* C. O. Paullin, *Atlas of the Historical Geography of the United States* (Washington: Carnegie Institution, 1932), plate 79b.

with the expansion of the railroad network, farming moved westward on a broad front, and fertile new lands in the Dakotas, Nebraska, Kansas, Oklahoma, Texas, and the Far West all contributed to an unprecedented outpouring of agricultural products. In the twentieth century technological progress alone would conquer diminishing returns in agriculture; but in the nineteenth century, when the pace of technological progress was slower and population growth more rapid, the availability of a vast expanse of unoccupied land played a crucial role in permitting economic growth to continue unhampered by the drag of diminishing returns.

It might be asked: why do we discuss land under the heading "Material Capital Accumulation"? After all, isn't land a "natural" resource? The answer is that land lies virtually useless to men in its natural state, and it yields its fruits only after human effort has turned it into a productive resource. Virgin soil is lush with weeds, brush, and wild flowers, but the market for these is exceedingly limited. Before it can yield wheat, corn, or cotton it must be cleared, plowed, cultivated, and often drained, fenced, or irrigated. To make the land useful we must invest in it, and the product of our efforts, *improved land*, is no less capital than is a drill press or a lathe. Like other forms of material capital, the stock of improved land can be augmented. Even trees and minerals are typically useless as they exist in nature; before they can assume a value trees must be cut, minerals dug, both transported to markets.[5] It is easy to exaggerate the significance of "natural" resources. America's immense territory yielded its riches only in response to human effort, and very little was obtained as a gift of nature.

Of course, if a territory lacks coal, no amount of effort or ingenuity will suffice to dig it up. But given the effort and ingenuity, lack of a particular "natural" resource would not matter much, for a good substitute would probably be soon provided. In any case, resources are useful only because the technology describes how to use them, and when a particular resource is relatively scarce—and hence relatively expensive—inventors are presented with a strong incentive to conceive of a good substitute material or a way of economizing on the material even in the absence of a good substitute. Ultimately the influence of the natural resource endowment on economic growth must yield to the much greater influence of technological ingenuity. And as we have already seen, the technological virtuosity of a population in a market economy depends crucially on the way property rights are defined and enforced.

[5] Recreational uses of resources constitute exceptions to these statements, but such uses were of little consequence during the post-Civil War era.

As the labor force and the quantity of improved land increased, the stock of structures and equipment more than kept pace. During the period from 1869 to World War I, this capital stock increased at an annual rate of about 4 percent. Since the labor force grew more slowly, the stock of material capital per worker increased steadily (Table 2.3).

TABLE 2.3
MATERIAL CAPITAL STOCK

Year	Total Material Capital Stock Net of Capital Consumption (Billions of 1929 Dollars)	Total Material Capital Stock Net of Capital Consumption per Member of Labor Force (Thousands of 1929 Dollars)
1869	27	2.11
1879	42	2.49
1889	68	3.06
1899	108	3.79
1909	165	4.41

SOURCE. Simon Kuznets, *Capital in the American Economy, Its Formation and Financing* (Princeton, N. J.: Princeton University, 1961), p. 64.

In the late 1870's the proportion of the national output being channeled into material investment was already quite high, in excess of 20 percent on a gross basis—including investment for maintaining the material capital stock as it wears out or becomes obsolete—and about 13 percent on a net basis. These ratios remained high throughout the period; during the decade 1899–1908 the gross material investment ratio was about 28 percent. Before 1860 the bulk of material investment had been in structures, but the relative importance of these declined steadily, while equipment became a larger element—evidence of the increasing extent to which production was being mechanized in the post-Civil War era. A substantial share of the material investment of this period went toward building the railroad network, especially during the 1870's and 1880's. Figures showing miles of main track (Table 2.4) give a rough indication of the expansion of the railroad system. The enormous growth of cities also provided major opportunities for profitable additions to the stock of structures and equipment.

TABLE 2.4

MILES OF MAIN RAILROAD TRACK

Year	Mileage
1869	46,800
1879	86,600
1889	161,300
1899	190,000
1909	238,100

SOURCE. Albert Fishlow, "Productivity and Technological Change in the Railroad Sector, 1840–1910," in National Bureau of Economic Research, Conference on Research in Income and Wealth, *Output, Employment, and Productivity in the United States after 1800* (New York: Columbia University, 1966), p. 596.

Human Capital Accumulation

The useful skills of the labor force constitute an important part of the nation's capital stock. Literacy, the most basic of these skills, was always widespread in the United States. In 1870 about 90 percent of adult white Americans could read and write; by 1910, 95 percent possessed these basic skills. For obvious reasons, literacy was much less prevalent among the nonwhite population—predominantly blacks—but improvement was rapid. In 1870 only about 20 percent of the adult nonwhite population was literate; by 1910 the proportion had increased to 70 percent. The erstwhile slaves apparently believed from the very start of their free existence that investment in education would yield a relatively high rate of return. That their property rights in human capital were less easily expropriated than their property rights in material capital may help to explain the blacks' rapid rate of advance in literacy.

For the nation as a whole, formal education progressed erratically. The school enrollment rate tended slightly upward, from 48 percent of school-aged (5–19 years old) children in 1870 to 59 percent in 1910, but reversals beset the advance. From 1880 to 1900 the enrollment rate fell substantially, from 58 to 51 percent, and then recovered in the first decade of the new century. We must interpret these figures cautiously, for actual attendance at schools fell substantially below enrollment, typically by as much as a third. The average student actually attended school no more than three or four months each year. The quality of the instruction was poor, teachers frequently being trained only marginally better than their students. Teenage girls formed a major part of the teaching staff, but marriage usually removed them from the job after a few years. Teachers' salaries were relatively low; in rural districts they often earned less than common laborers.

Impressed by such evidence, one scholar has ventured the judgment that, considering the quantity and the quality of formal education in the nineteenth century, "Taken together they do not suggest that formal education was anything like a significant factor in raising the quality of the American labor force, or in stimulating economic growth."[6] In a fundamental sense, however, this judgment may miss the point. Economic growth is the return on mutually interdependent investments; we cannot neglect the *complementarity* among skilled workers, mechanization, and advancing technology. Growth simply cannot be sustained for long where the bulk of the population is illiterate and unskilled. In the United States illiteracy never obstructed economic progress. And not only was the labor force mostly literate, but an increasing number of workers invested in acquiring additional skills as the tasks to be performed grew more complex and intellectually demanding. In 1870 only about 2 percent of those at least 17 years old had graduated from high school, but in 1914 the proportion exceeded 10 percent. The number of bachelor's degrees conferred increased from about 10,000 in 1870 to over 44,000 in 1914, and in the latter year the nation's universities also granted more than 3000 master's and over 550 doctor's degrees. Of course these data measure only very imperfectly the formation of human capital, for much education is consumption rather than investment. Yet the evidence suggests quite strongly that the economically useful skills of the average worker did improve and did contribute toward raising the productivity of labor. The question remains: how much growth can be explained in this way? Unfortunately, a firm answer must await the results of future study.

Albert Fishlow's research indicates that the nation channeled an increasing proportion of its resources into the production of formal education during the nineteenth century (Table 2.5). Merely adding the amounts spent to provide school buildings and to pay teachers' salaries does not give a complete account of the cost of education. Whether education is viewed from the point of view of the individual student or from that of society, there is an additional cost: the earnings the student foregoes when he occupies himself with studies instead of some alternative productive occupation. This opportunity cost, which was substantial under nineteenth-century conditions of widespread child labor, has been taken into account in arriving at the "total resource cost" figures of Table 2.5. The table also shows that while public education expanded progressively, private education provided a substantial

[6] Stanley Lebergott, "Labor Force and Employment, 1800–1960," in National Bureau of Economic Research, Conference on Research in Income and Wealth, *Output, Employment, and Productivity in the United States after 1800* (New York: Columbia University, 1966), p. 126.

TABLE 2.5

COSTS OF EDUCATION

Fiscal Year	Direct Expenditures (Millions of Current Dollars)	Public Outlays (Millions of Current Dollars)	Total Resource Costs (Millions of Current Dollars)	Direct Expenditures Relative to GNP	Total Resource Costs Relative to GNP
1860	35	20	60	0.008	0.014
1870	95	62		0.013	
1880	106	82	181	0.011	0.018
1890	187	147		0.015	
1900	290	230	503	0.017	0.029

SOURCE. Albert Fishlow, "Levels of Nineteenth-Century American Investment in Education," *Journal of Economic History*, XXVI (Dec. 1966), 430.

share during the early years and still supplied more than 20 percent in 1900. Catholics and Lutherans led in supplying private education.

Workers acquired a large part of their skills not at schools but on the job. Skilled craftsmen—carpenters, masons, blacksmiths, coopers, wheelwrights, printers, mechanics, and many others—typically gained their skills through apprenticeships. The same was true of engineers, lawyers, and physicians. Without doubt, practically all farming skills were transmitted on the farm, often within the family. These kinds of training clearly constitute investment in human capital, but the available evidence is insufficient to indicate the rates at which they were increasing. On-the-job training, however, might well have been more important than formal education during the post-Civil War era. Despite its importance, this subject has yet to be systematically studied.

Health, like education, is a form of capital, but not until near the end of the nineteenth century did Americans make substantial investments in improving their health. Though probably superior to contemporary European standards, American health conditions in the mid-nineteenth century were by present-day standards almost unbelievably poor. Disastrous epidemics occurred frequently—yellow fever, smallpox, cholera, typhoid, diphtheria, and typhus were common scourges. As if these periodic afflictions were not enough, a very substantial part of the population suffered from chronic diseases. Hookworm disease plagued the people of the South. Malaria and dysentery, also prevalent there, spread throughout the great interior basin drained by the Mississippi River system, where the people complained resignedly of the "ague," and every autumn saw a new onslaught of "fevers." Tuberculosis, the greatest killer of all, flourished in the rapidly expanding cities. Disease not only took a heavy toll in human lives, but in addition it frequently left the survivors in a debilitated and less productive condition.

The conditions that fostered frequent illness are easily identified. Perhaps the first thing noticed by a modern man, could he be projected back in time-machine fashion to the mid-nineteenth century, would be the ubiquitous filth. Cities were probably more objectionable than the countryside, as evidenced by a physician's vivid description of New York's slums in 1865:

> Domestic garbage and filth of every kind is thrown into the streets, covering their surface, filling the gutters, obstructing the sewer culverts, and sending forth perennial emanations which must generate pestiferous disease. In winter the filth and garbage, etc., accumulate in the streets to the depth sometimes of two or three feet.
>
> The refuse of the bedrooms of those sick with typhoid and scarlet fevers and smallpox is frequently thrown into the streets, there to contaminate the air, and, no doubt, aid in the spread of those pestilential diseases.
>
> At high tide the water often wells up through the floors [of the cellar apartments occupied by some 18,000 New Yorkers], submerging them to a considerable depth. In very many cases the vaults of privies are situated on the same or a higher level, and their contents frequently ooze through the walls into the occupied apartments beside them.[7]

Conscious design could hardly have produced conditions more agreeable to the spread of infectious diseases, and the cost of living amid such filth was a sickly and uncertain existence. But although the stench and ugliness sometimes gave rise to complaints, the connection between filth and disease escaped widespread recognition.

Until near the end of the century the causes of almost all diseases remained shrouded in mystery, and hence no really effective steps could be taken to combat them. Medical science, lacking a tested theory of infection, could do very little to relieve the suffering; more often its false cures exacerbated the afflictions of the sick. The most popular theory, that of miasmatic contagion, maintained that disease results from the breathing of air contaminated by the vapors rising from decomposing animal and vegetable matter. (The New York physician quoted above obviously subscribed to this theory.) Interestingly, this false theory did lead to some improvements in public health, for it prescribed the construction of sewers and the removal of garbage from the streets, which

[7] Cited in C.-E. A. Winslow, *The Evolution and Significance of the Modern Public Health Campaign* (New Haven: Yale University, 1923), p. 10.

reduced the spread of certain diseases. The backwardness of formal medical science probably made little difference, for most physicians were untrained anyhow. A Swedish immigrant recorded with surprise: "A person I have seen going about working as a mason served for a couple of months as an assistant in a drug store in Milwaukee, whereupon he laid aside the trowel, got himself some medical books, and assumed the title of doctor."[8] The nineteenth century abounded in such curious examples of recruitment into the medical profession. Throughout most of the century only two serious diseases responded to the usual treatments: smallpox to vaccination, and malaria to quinine. As late as 1860, "bleed and purge" remained the most common prescription for the treatment of serious disease. Naturally, such remedies destroyed many who would otherwise have survived.

Toward the end of the century the discoveries of Louis Pasteur, Robert Koch, and their followers made possible the first effective campaign against infectious diseases. These scientists showed that many diseases result from the action of microorganisms, bacteria, and that these can be destroyed by substances toxic to them but not to the human organism itself. Within a few years bacteriologists had identified the specific microorganisms responsible for many ailments. In a few cases vaccines were developed to combat the diseases, but of much greater significance was the impetus given to measures designed to impede the transmission of infectious agents. Armed for the first time with firm knowledge about infectious disease causation and transmission, cities devoted increasing amounts of resources to sewage disposal and treatment, the pasteurization of milk, and the provision of pure water. The number of urban people drinking filtered water increased from 30,000 in 1880 to over 20,000,000 in 1920.[9]

These investments in better health yielded returns in several ways. One measure of the improvements in health is the falling death rate. In New York, Boston, Philadelphia, and New Orleans, taken together, the death rate stood at 30 in 1840–1864, at 26 in 1865–1889, and at 19 in 1890–1914.[10] For the nation as a whole the death rate declined from about 23 in the 1870's to about 15 in 1915. After 1900 great epidemics became increasingly rare and finally nonexistent. Life expectancy at birth increased

[8] Cited in Stanley Lebergott, *Manpower in Economic Growth* (New York: McGraw-Hill, 1964), p. 120.

[9] George C. Whipple, "Fifty Years of Water Purification," in Mazyck P. Ravenel, Ed., *A Half Century of Public Health* (New York: American Public Health Association, 1921), p. 166.

[10] Frederick L. Hoffman, "American Mortality Progress During the Last Half Century," in Ravenel, *op. cit.*, p. 102.

substantially: in Massachusetts, for which reliable data exist, it rose from about 40 years in 1855 to more than 50 on the eve of the Great War; and fragmentary evidence suggests that the improvement was at least as great elsewhere. That people lived longer and endured less physical pain cannot be doubted. And since many of these improvements worked mainly to reduce child mortality, the sorrow of losing children was diminished and the cost of fruitless pregnancies more often avoided. These improvements in health are surely one of the most significant welfare gains to accompany economic growth.

Organizational Changes and Economies of Scale

In a market economy the fundamental unit of economic organization is the business firm, of which there are three basic kinds according to ownership: the single proprietorship, the partnership, and the corporation. Each has characteristic advantages and might be preferred to the others under certain circumstances. The single proprietorship generally prevails where the scale of operations is small. It allows the owner to have complete control over his business, to operate it as he thinks best. Financial difficulties often arise, however, when a single owner wishes to expand his business; the partnership then becomes attractive. The necessity for mutual trust limits the number of partners. If the business becomes so large by the addition of new partners that no one can keep track of its condition, all may come to grief, because each partner's legal liability extends to his personal property as well as to that invested in the firm. In addition, the limited life-span of the partners increases the risks of creditors who lend to the partnership, and consequently the business can borrow only at relatively high rates of interest. The corporate form of organization solves the interrelated problems of size, liability, and longevity inherent in the partnership. The corporation can usually obtain funds by selling its stocks—ownership shares in the firm—to the public. Investors often subscribe to such securities even without a detailed knowledge of the firm's operations because each risks only the amount of his subscription. Unlike the simpler forms of organization, the corporation lives on when all of its original shareholders have died, because the stocks can be passed on to heirs or sold without disrupting the organization of the firm.

Before the Civil War the organization of economic life had been relatively uncomplicated. Most businessmen conducted their affairs within small and highly localized markets, and therefore proprietorships and partnerships predominated. The few existing corporations appeared in industries where the "public interest" intruded, such as turnpikes, railroads, banks, insurance, and utilities. Although several surges of incorporation occurred before the Civil War, the corporation did little more than hold its own with the other forms of business organization.

After the war, incorporation increased greatly, and although the number of incorporations typically fell during business depressions the trend was sharply upward for the next half century. Incorporations of financial firms and utilities declined relatively, while manufacturing incorporations became more prevalent. During the two decades from the mid-1870's to the mid-1890's entrepreneurs adopted the corporation in many fields where it had not previously appeared. After the 1890's the incorporation of trade and service businesses became progressively more common.[11]

The rise of the corporation reflected several influences. One was the increasing size of markets. As firms expanded to meet a growing demand, they typically found it desirable to assume the corporate form, for reasons already discussed. Another influence was the development of formal markets for corporate stocks and bonds, which reduced the costs of attracting new investors in corporate securities. Changes in the law also encouraged incorporation. As early as 1816 the legislatures of Connecticut and New Hampshire had passed statutes providing for limited liability, thus resolving a long-unsettled legal question, and by 1860 this provision was widespread among the states. In the early part of the century, incorporation had typically required a special charter granted by a state legislature, which explains why so many corporations then bore a close relation to the "public interest." Although some states had passed general incorporation acts early in the century—for example, New York in 1811—not until the 1870's did constitutionally required incorporation under general laws become the rule in most states. Under these laws, entrepreneurs could incorporate their firms simply by filing a few papers and paying a small fee. The costs of incorporation being greatly reduced, increasing numbers of businessmen selected this form of organization. By 1916 more than 340,000 corporations had been formed, over 80,000 of them in manufacturing.

An economy in which the corporation is the most important form of business organization is certain to differ in fundamental respects from one in which proprietorships and partnerships prevail: fewer people are self-employed, and more are wage earners; firms are larger, more impersonal, and more bureaucratic; even political power may come to rest with those who control the large corporations. These are important consequences,

[11] For detailed statistics concerning incorporation, see George Heberton Evans, Jr., *Business Incorporations in the United States, 1800–1943* (New York: National Bureau of Economic Research, 1948).

but our present concern is with the corporation's relation to economic growth. The question is whether the rise of the corporation led to increased productivity, and the answer is that it did.

The crucial link between greater efficiency and incorporation is size. As we have seen, firms normally assumed the corporate form in order to facilitate their expansion. But expansion did not mean simply producing more in the same way, for larger firms could frequently make use of improved forms of organization that enabled them to reduce the average cost of production. Larger size permitted greater specialization of functions within the firm, which promoted efficiency. A famous novel, written in 1905, gives a graphic description of the efficiency that resulted from the division of labor in the meat-packing industry:

> The carcass hog was scooped out of the vat by machinery, and then it fell to the second floor, passing on the way through a wonderful machine with numerous scrapers, which adjusted themselves to the size and shape of the animal, and sent it out at the other end with nearly all of its bristles removed. It was then again strung up by machinery, and sent upon another trolley ride; this time passing between two lines of men, who sat upon a raised platform, each doing a certain single thing to the carcass as it came to him. One scraped the outside of a leg; another scraped the inside of the same leg. One with a swift stroke cut the throat; another with two swift strokes severed the head, which fell to the floor and vanished through a hole. Another made a slit down the body; a second opened the body wider; a third with a saw cut the breastbone, a fourth loosened the entrails; a fifth pulled them out—and they also slid through a hole in the floor. There were men to scrape each side and men to scrape the back; there were men to clean the carcass inside, to trim it and wash it. Looking down this room one saw, creeping slowly, a line of dangling hogs a hundred yards in length; and for every yard there was a man, working as if a demon were after him.[12]

The use of more efficient techniques requiring highly indivisible, or "lumpy," capital goods like bristle-scraping machines or conveyers was advantageous only when large outputs were produced. An assembly line like the one described above was economical only for packers handling hundreds, perhaps thousands, of animals each day. In sum, incorporation allowed firms to grow, and growth often permitted the realization of various economies of scale, thus raising productivity.

Besides the rise of the corporation, numerous other organizational changes occurred during the post-Civil War era. The merger movement, for example, reached a crest around the turn of the century. Mergers often led to greater productivity; in Alfred Chandler's words,

[12] Upton Sinclair, *The Jungle* (New York: Signet Classics, 1960), pp. 40–41.

> The transformation of a loose alliance of manufacturing or marketing firms into a single consolidated organization with a central headquarters made possible economies of scale through standardization of processes and standardization in the procurement of materials. Of more significance, consolidation permitted a concentration of production in a few large favorably located factories. By handling a high volume of output, consolidated factories reduced the cost of making each individual unit. They could specialize further and subdivide the process of manufacturing and also were often able to develop and apply new technological improvements more easily than could smaller units. To a lesser extent consolidations of marketing firms offered comparable advantages.[13]

Expansion of the market led to greater specialization and hence to higher productivity *within* individual firms, as described above, but economies of scale also appeared in a broader context. In a growing market many firms themselves became more and more specialized. For example, in the early nineteenth century, textile manufacturers produced their own equipment, for the total demand for such machinery was too small in any particular place to support a firm specializing in such products, and transportation charges were too high to permit an economical centralization of machinery production. As the demand for textiles became larger, the demand for textile machinery also increased, and about the middle of the century specialized machinery producers began to appear. This specialization *among* firms raised productivity throughout the textile industry, for it enabled the machinery firms to benefit from the learning process inherent in specialization and then, through competition with one another, to pass benefits on to textile makers in the form of reduced machinery costs. In a similar fashion countless other new industries emerged. Of special significance was the appearance of a distinct industry producing machine tools, instruments for cutting, grinding, and polishing metals. This became a focus for the discovery and dissemination of new techniques applicable to a wide range of manufacturing processes.[14]

The costs of transacting exchanges fell in most markets during this period. For example, the financial markets, where savings are channeled into investment, became more efficient on a national scale as funds began to flow more freely between regions. In a growing market a host of spe-

[13] Alfred D. Chandler, Jr., *Strategy and Structure: Chapters in the History of the Industrial Enterprise* (Cambridge, Mass.: M. I. T. Press, 1962), p. 37.

[14] On the strategic role of the machine tool industry in economic growth, see Nathan Rosenberg, "Capital Goods, Technology, and Economic Growth," *Oxford Economic Papers,* XV (Nov. 1963), and *idem,* "Technological Change in the Machine Tool Industry, 1840–1910," *Journal of Economic History,* XXIII (Dec. 1963).

cialists—brokers, investment bankers, financial journalists, and others—arose to perform services, typically involving the collection and dissemination of information, enabling the market system to operate more efficiently as a by-product of their own pursuit of wealth.

Technological Progress

Technological progress means an increase in useful knowledge. It is useful to think of it as occurring in three steps: (1) invention, the original conception of a new idea; (2) innovation, its original application in a firm's production process; and (3) diffusion, its spread from the innovator to applications in other firms. Some inventions never become innovations, and some innovations never spread beyond their original application. The diffusion of a new idea may require many years, or even decades. Very often new knowledge is applicable only in conjunction with a new capital good; economists then speak of technological progress as "embodied" in the material capital. Because of this embodiment, material capital accumulation takes on an additional productivity-raising dimension. Not only does it augment the productivity of labor by increasing the material capital/labor ratio, but it provides as well a vehicle for the implementation of new ideas, for raising the intellectual capital/labor ratio. The examples of technological progress considered below comprise only a minute sample from a vast universe. We must remember, too, that major productivity gains often resulted from a series of minor improvements. The spectacular technological advance captures everyone's attention, but ultimately the small, unspectacular advances may have had an even greater importance.

The steamboat revolutionized inland transportation in the early nineteenth century, and in combination with the canals it gave the United States a transportation system that compared favorably with those of the advanced European nations. The two decades before the Civil War were the golden age of the steamboat, but beginning in the 1840's the railroad, which had first appeared in the United States in 1830, began to furnish serious competition for the water carriers. By 1860 the railroads operated over 30,000 miles of main lines. The railroad was much less an improvement over the steamboats than the steamboats had been over flatboats, keelboats, and wagons. Still, the iron horse progressively displaced water transportation in most lines. Mark Twain portrayed the trend in a characteristic description:

> Boat used to land—captain on hurricane roof—mighty stiff and straight—iron ramrod for a spine—kid gloves, plug tile, hair parted behind—man on shore takes off hat and says—

> "Got twenty-eight tons of wheat, cap'n—be great favor if you can take them."
>
> " 'll take two of them"—and don't even condescend to look at him.
>
> But now-a-days the captain takes off his old slouch, and smiles all the way around to the back of his ears, and gets off a bow which he hasn't got any ramrod to interfere with, and says—
>
> "Glad to see you, Smith, glad to see you—you're looking well—haven't seen you looking so well for years—what you got for us?"
>
> "Nuth'n," says Smith; and keeps his hat on, and just turns his back and goes to talking with somebody else.[15]

The water carriers, being relatively more efficient in the carriage of bulky, low-value-per-pound goods, survived and even flourished transporting grains, ores, and coal. After the Civil War the development of towboat-barge systems helped the river carriers to retain much of their business on the Ohio and the Mississippi, and enormous ore boats on the Great Lakes continued to expand their trade. But the future belonged to the railroad, and its impact was so great that some historians have dubbed the post-Civil War era the Railway Age. Probably no other single invention in the nineteenth century had such far-reaching influence.

Railroads did not simply provide more cheaply the same service that canals and steamboats had previously supplied. In fact, transport rates on the canals, lakes, and rivers, in cents per ton-mile, remained lower than railroad rates. But the railroad provided a service so superior in quality that it more than compensated for its higher price. Its major advantages were more direct routes, reduced transshipment, greater speed and safety, and year-round service. With the introduction of the railroad, insurance rates and warehousing charges fell, as did the degree of uncertainty surrounding shipping and delivery dates. Commerce became more predictable. Moreover, the railroad permitted the settlement of large parts of the western United States where water transportation was not feasible, and there its influence was most striking. The availability of railroad transportation in the trans-Mississippi West encouraged a far-reaching relocation of agricultural activities; grain and meat production soon concentrated in this area. This relocation contributed substantially toward raising overall agricultural productivity.[16]

15 Mark Twain, *Life on the Mississippi* (New York: Charles L. Webster, 1891), pp. 570–71.

16 For calculations of the effect of the westward movement on productivity in grain cultivation, see William N. Parker and Judith L. V. Klein, "Productivity Growth in Grain Production in the United States, 1840–60 and 1900–10," in National Bureau of Economic Research, Conference on Research in Income and Wealth, *Output, Employment, and Productivity in the United States after 1800* (New York: Columbia University, 1966).

In communications great technological advances occurred. The telegraph had appeared in the 1840's; the telephone followed in the 1870's; and both continued to diffuse, supplying progressively more services. Information could now be transmitted in seconds instead of days. The availability of instant communications improved the working of markets by increasing their competitiveness, for traders could now carry out arbitrage operations quickly—buying in one market to sell in another with higher prices—thus insuring that prices in different markets for the same good would normally differ only by the cost of transportation between the places. Businessmen could discover opportunities for remunerative sales in markets throughout the nation. David A. Wells noted in 1889 that "the command through the telegraph of instantaneous information throughout the world of the conditions and prospects of all markets for all commodities has also undoubtedly operated to impart steadiness to prices, increase the safety of mercantile and manufacturing operations, and reduce the elements of speculation and of panics to the lowest minimum."[17] In short, the telephone and the telegraph lowered the cost of information and thereby contributed toward increasing productivity throughout the entire economic system by reducing the uncertainties surrounding transactions and by reducing the quantity of resources committed to search activities or tied up in inventory stocks. On the eve of World War I, Western Union handled more than 100 million telegraphic messages annually, and over 10 million telephones facilitated additional communications.

Technological advances in agriculture, where a large proportion of the nation's total output originated, had a major influence in determining the economy's overall rate of productivity growth. Improved iron and steel plows, cultivators, seed drills, reapers, and threshing machines had all appeared before the Civil War, but their diffusion continued for decades after 1865. A variety of horse-drawn implements like the spring-tooth and disc harrows, the gang plow, the self-binding reaper, and the "combine" reaper-thresher appeared after the war. These examples illustrate "embodied" technological progress. Other advances, like new methods of plowing and crop rotation, were "disembodied," not requiring new capital goods for their implementation. Livestock keepers improved the quality of their animals through selective breeding, and farmers raised the quality of their crops by carefully selecting hardier, more disease-resistant seeds. After 1905 the gasoline tractor came into use, giving indications of even greater productivity gains in agriculture that would come with the replacement of horsepower by the internal combustion engine.

[17] David A. Wells, *Recent Economic Changes* (New York: Appleton, 1889), p. 82.

Sweeping technological advances occurred in manufacturing. The sewing machine, invented in the 1840's, was put to varied use in the garment and shoe industries as well as in homes. In the 1870's the milling industry adopted roller grinding, which allowed the transformation of hard Western wheats into fine, high-quality flour. Refrigerated railway cars and storage rooms made meatpacking and fresh meat distribution into a unified national industry after 1880, putting fresh meat from the Midwest on the tables of consumers throughout the nation. The Bessemer converter and the open-hearth process revolutionized the steel industry, permitting for the first time the large-scale manufacture of steel at prices

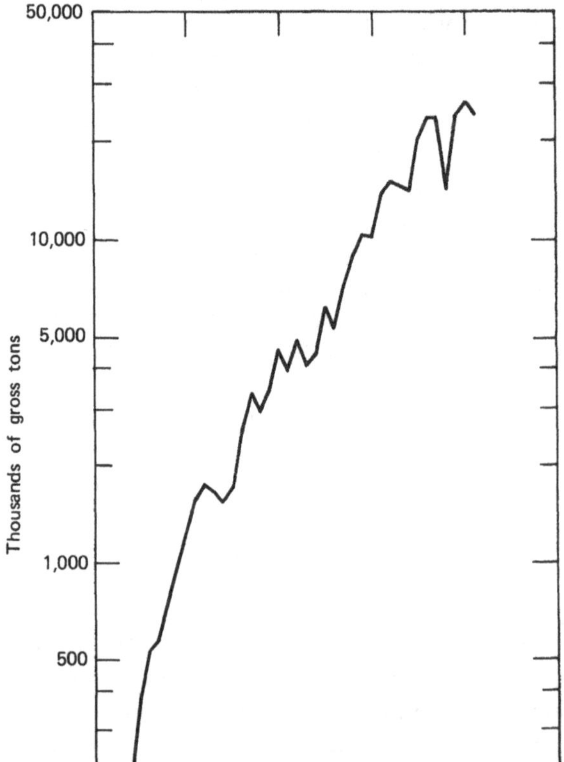

Figure 2.7 Steel production. *Source:* Peter Temin, *Iron and Steel in Nineteenth-Century America* (Cambridge, Mass.: M. I. T. Press, 1964), pp. 270–71.

so low that it soon became commonly used as a building material throughout industry (Figure 2.7). Steel makers made major productivity gains by rearranging their plants to eliminate much of the reheating of materials and to capture valuable by-products. The productivity of machine tools increased rapidly. High-speed tool steel—an alloy that retains its strength at high temperatures—appeared around the turn of the century, permitting cutting operations to be performed much quicker. During the 1870's steam surpassed water as a source of power, and after 1890 electrical power was increasingly applied in industrial uses. Between 1865 and 1915 aggregate energy consumption increased more than fivefold, and mineral fuels (predominantly coal), which had provided less than 20 percent of this energy in 1865, furnished over 85 percent in 1915.

MAIN PATTERNS OF TRANSFORMATION

The composition of the economy's total output changed dramatically in the post-Civil War era (Table 2.6). As their incomes rose, consumers in-

TABLE 2.6

PERCENTAGE DISTRIBUTION OF COMMODITY OUTPUT

Year	Agriculture	Mining	Manufacturing	Construction
1869	53	2	33	12
1874	46	2	39	12
1879	49	3	37	11
1884	41	3	44	12
1889	37	4	48	11
1894	32	4	53	11
1899	33	5	53	9

SOURCE. Robert E. Gallman, "Commodity Output, 1839–1899," in National Bureau of Economic Research, Conference on Research in Income and Wealth, *Trends in the American Economy in the Nineteenth Century* (Princeton, N. J.: Princeton University, 1960), p. 26.

creased their spending for the products of agriculture only slowly, and for manufactured products much more rapidly. Moreover, the rise in the fraction of total income used to finance material investment placed a greater demand on the manufacturing industries. As a result, the rate of return in manufacturing enterprises became relatively greater, and entrepreneurs moved to expand such production; at the same time many farmers, discouraged by their relative lack of success, sought to improve their condition by seeking nonfarm occupations. The upshot of these movements was the transformation of a predominantly agrarian economy into a great industrial economy—a transformation so sweeping and pregnant with implications that economic historians have called it an "industrial revolution" and made it the focus of a major part of their research for the past century. In 1870, after several decades of industrial growth, the United States had a manufacturing output equal to that of France and Germany combined, but only about three fourths as large as that of the United Kingdom; by 1913 the American manufacturing output equalled that of France, Germany, and the United Kingdom combined! Still the greatest producer of raw materials and foodstuffs, the United States had become the world's industrial giant as well.

The rapid growth of manufacturing, trade, and transportation outputs and the relative decline of agricultural output led to parallel changes in the distribution of employment among the various sectors (Table 2.7).

TABLE 2.7

PERCENTAGE DISTRIBUTION OF LABOR FORCE

Year	Farming, Fishing, and Mining	Construction	Manufacturing	Trade	Ocean and Rail Transport	Domestics
1870	54	6	19	10	2	8
1880	53	5	19	11	3	7
1890	45	7	19	13	4	7
1900	43	6	20	14	4	6
1910	34	5	22	14	5	6

SOURCE. Stanley Lebergott, "Labor Force and Employment, 1800–1960," in National Bureau of Economic Research, Conference on Research in Income and Wealth, *Output, Employment, and Productivity in the United States after 1800* (New York: Columbia University, 1966), p. 119.

Most striking was the great reduction in the agricultural share: in 1870 well over half of all workers were farmers or farm laborers; by 1910 only one in three was. The relative employment gains, being spread over several sectors, were less obvious than agriculture's relative losses. Transportation employment grew fastest of all, trade employment somewhat slower; and the still slower expansion of manufacturing jobs seems really quite moderate in relation to the immense outpouring of manufactured goods. The relatively slow expansion of manufacturing employment is partly a statistical illusion arising from changes in the definition of manufacturing workers starting with the census of 1900, but to a larger extent it reflects the enormous increases in output per worker achieved in the manufacturing sector.

While the sectoral composition of output and employment underwent rapid changes, locational patterns shifted in an equally radical way. The thrust of the interregional movement was westward, but the pattern was more complicated than this simple statement suggests (Table 2.8).

TABLE 2.8

PERCENTAGE REGIONAL DISTRIBUTION OF POPULATION

Year	New England	Middle Atlantic	East North Central	West North Central	South Atlantic	East South Central	West South Central	Mountain	Pacific
1870	9	25	24	10	12	11	5	1	2
1880	8	23	22	12	13	11	7	1	2
1890	8	22	22	14	12	10	8	2	3
1900	7	22	21	14	12	10	9	2	3
1910	7	23	20	13	11	9	10	3	5

SOURCE. Richard A. Easterlin, "Interregional Differences in Per Capita Income, Population, and Total Income, 1840–1950," in National Bureau of Economic Research, Conference on Research in Income and Wealth, *Trends in the American Economy in the Nineteenth Century* (Princeton, N. J.: Princeton University, 1960), p. 136. Percentages may not sum to 100 because of rounding. Regions are defined as follows. *New England*: Maine, Vermont, New Hampshire, Massachusetts, Connecticut, and Rhode Island. *Middle Atlantic*: New York, New Jersey, Pennsylvania, Delaware, and Maryland. *East North Central*: Ohio, Indiana, Illinois, Michigan, and Wisconsin. *West North Central*: Minnesota, Iowa, Missouri, North Dakota, South Dakota, Nebraska, and Kansas. *South Atlantic*: Virginia, West Virginia, North Carolina, South Carolina, Georgia, and Florida. *East South Central*: Kentucky, Tennessee, Alabama, and Mississippi. *West South Central*: Arkansas, Louisiana, Oklahoma, and Texas. *Mountain*: Montana, Idaho, Wyoming, Colorado, New Mexico, Arizona, Utah, and Nevada. *Pacific*: Washington, Oregon, and California.

In general, opportunities for earning an income determined the locations of productive activities, and individual workers and businessmen adjusted accordingly, though population movements did of course produce a feedback effect on decisions about the location of production. The overall impression of scholars who have studied migration patterns is that Americans moved readily in an attempt to improve their economic condition. This high mobility played an important role in the successful functioning of a geographically vast market economy.

A DIGRESSION: HOW GROWTH BEGAN

> Capital formation is one of the conditions of economic growth, and the existence of a law of property is one of the conditions of capital formation. . . . For if a resource and its fruit could not be protected against the public at large, it would certainly be misused, and hardly any person would find it worth while to invest in its improvement. . . . [U]nless we match differential effort with differential reward, men are unlikely to take the trouble to develop their talents and resources to the utmost of their capabilities.
>
> W. ARTHUR LEWIS

Economic growth did not begin with a great leap after the Civil War. Although our evidence on when it actually began is scanty, it appears certain that rapid growth occurred in the two decades before the Civil War, and output per capita probably increased also in the two decades before 1840, although at a slower rate. In short, sustained economic growth began sometime in the first half of the nineteenth century. Perhaps the attempt to date the starting point with any greater precision is really not a fruitful exercise. After all, economic growth did not just suddenly appear; rather, it emerged slowly and haltingly, against many obstacles and with many temporary setbacks.

In a book concerned only with the post-Civil War era, we could easily dismiss the subject of how growth began as a question belonging to another study. But that would be a serious mistake, for unless we understand how growth began, we cannot really understand how it continued in a self-sustaining fashion throughout the post-Civil War era. In this digression, we offer a theory of how growth began. Though we shall present some evidence that it is consistent with the facts of American economic history, no rigorous tests of the hypotheses implied by this theory are presently available. Property rights, which play a central role in the theory, are particularly difficult to incorporate into clear-cut hypothesis tests. Our hope is that by sketching the theory we will encourage others to join in the attempt to extend and test it. Having issued our caveats at the outset, we proceed below without qualification.

Before the nineteenth century, relatively little investment in material capital took place, the technology advanced haltingly, and workers acquired new skills at a snail's pace. This virtual absence of productivity-raising activities, extending back through millenia of civilized history, sprang from two sources.

The first was the prevalence of limited markets. The limitations on the effective size of markets arose in some places from small populations, in other places from low levels of income per capita, and in most places from both. Primitive technologies of transportation and communication obstructed the widening of effective markets through interregional or international trade, and high costs of information about potential foreign markets restricted trade to items with high value/weight ratios, as in the famous medieval spice trade. With the revival of commerce in the late medieval period, European markets began to widen; population growth promoted the same result. But these changes occurred slowly, ever so slowly, and with frequent reversals as wars and raiding disrupted trade and as plagues, famines, and other natural disasters decimated the population of Europe. Over the centuries, however, markets did grow, the settlement of North America by English colonists being a simple overseas extension of this growth. The colonies expanded in response to the home country's growing demand for American staples—tobacco, rice, indigo, fish, lumber, naval stores. Later, in the early nineteenth century, cotton became the leading export. The expansion of a rapidly growing population westward into an apparently inexhaustible area of fertile land made possible an increasing supply of these goods. Within the United States the growth of population from less than 4 million in 1790 to more than 31 million in 1860 provided visible evidence of widening markets. At the same time canals, steamboats, and railroads made the population more internally accessible. Certainly before the middle of the nineteenth century, narrow markets no longer constrained the undertaking of productivity-raising activities in America.[1]

[1] For a detailed account of the widening of markets in the early national period,

Large markets alone, however, could not stimulate many individuals to invent or to acquire skills. The second requirement was the development of secure private property rights, for even with wide markets the substantial risk remained that, having made investments in raising their productivity, investors would be unable to capture gains sufficient to justify the effort. The same insecurity influenced the accumulation of material capital where the returns accrued over a lengthy and uncertain future. As markets became geographically larger, with many transactions being necessarily conducted at a distance, the problems of insuring that one's property would be respected grew more severe. And always the threat was twofold, for property rights might be disregarded by governments as well as by other individuals. With private property rights ill-defined and ill-enforced, individuals could not form reliable expectations. Uncertainty dominated the future, and only the fool or the humanitarian risked valuable resources in ventures promising greater but later rewards.

Englishmen, of course, had proceeded further than others toward securing the rights of private property. But much remained to be done even in the late eighteenth century, and in many cases the American colonists enjoyed less protection than their cousins did at home. After all, the American Revolution was in large measure provoked by the British government's arbitrary treatment of American property. Mere independence, however, did not cure these ills completely. Shays' Rebellion, a 1786 uprising of Massachusetts farmers defying court orders to repay debts as agreed in their contracts, alarmed many throughout the new nation and intensified concern for the security of property. In November 1787, James Madison complained of a "prevailing and increasing distrust of public engagements, and alarm for private rights, which are echoed from one end of the continent to the other." And two months later he wrote:

> The sober people of America are weary of the fluctuating policy which has directed the public councils. They have seen with regret and indignation that sudden changes and legislative interferences, in cases affecting personal rights, become jobs in the hands of enterprising and influential speculators, and snares to the more-industrious and less-informed part of the community. They have seen, too, that one legislative interference is but the first link of a long chain of repetitions, every subsequent interference being naturally produced by the effects of the preceding. They very rightly infer, therefore, that some thorough reform is wanting, which

see Douglass C. North, *The Economic Growth of the United States, 1790–1860* (Englewood Cliffs, N. J.: Prentice-Hall, 1961).

will banish speculations on public measures, inspire a general prudence and industry, and give a regular course to the business of society.[2]

Independence did create an opportunity for Americans to establish a new framework of property rights consistent with their desire for material advancement. The Constitution was the first step, and in many ways the most important one. Its provisions for security against foreign and domestic threats, for post offices and roads, for duty-free interstate trade, and for uniform bankruptcy laws directly helped to promote trade and specialization. It also gave Congress the right to provide for a patent system: "To promote the progress of science and useful arts by securing for limited times to authors and inventors the exclusive right to their respective writings and discoveries." With greater assurance of capturing the gains from their ideas, inventors emerged more rapidly than ever before. Of immense importance was the provision prohibiting any state from passing a law that would impair the obligation of contracts. In 1819 John Marshall, Chief Justice of the U. S. Supreme Court, recalled the insecurity that had afflicted the rights of private property before the Constitution: "[A] course of legislation had prevailed in many, if not in all, of the states, which weakened the confidence of man in man, and embarrassed all transactions between individuals, by dispensing with a faithful performance of engagements." Marshall apparently had in mind the acts passed by seven states in the 1780's authorizing the issue of paper currency to serve as a legal tender for the settlement of debts contracted in terms of specie. The Contract Clause of the Constitution, he said, was designed "to correct this mischief, by restraining the power which produced it."[3] The Constitution also explicitly forbade the states to coin money or to emit bills of credit. The Bill of Rights, ten amendments to the Constitution adopted in 1791, guaranteed "the right of the people to be secure in their persons, houses, papers, and effects, against unreasonable searches and seizures"; it provided that no person "be deprived of life, liberty, or property, without due process of law; nor shall private property be taken for public use, without just compensation"; furthermore, "in Suits at common law, where the value in controversy shall exceed twenty dollars, the right of trial by jury shall be preserved." In brief, the Constitution laid the foundation of private property rights so as to curb the arbitrary powers of government and to promote the security required for the pursuit of productivity-raising activities of all kinds.

2 James Madison, in *The Federalist* (New York: Modern Library, n. d.), pp. 54, 289.

3 *Trustees of Dartmouth College v. Woodward* (1819), reprinted in Henry Steele Commager, Ed., *Documents of American History*, 4th ed. (New York: Appleton, Century, Crofts, 1948), pp. 220–23.

Upon this foundation an imposing legal structure arose in the first half of the nineteenth century. Of central importance were the elaboration and extension of the common law of contract. With English precedents as a starting point, judges set down new rules for the legal treatment of negotiable instruments like notes, bills of exchange and lading, and warehouse receipts. In an expanding and far-flung market, uniform standards for dealing with these commercial documents were essential. Judges also clarified the legal responsibilities of factors and agents and extended the law with respect to banking and insurance. In 1836 Congress reformed the patent system, and the new law, in combination with its subsequent interpretations by the courts, did much more to protect inventors' rights to their ideas. In all these areas the general effect was to facilitate the operation of private economic activities and to stabilize the expectations of individuals concerning the legal status of private property in its various forms. The doctrine of *stare decisis*—that lower courts are bound by the prior decision of the highest court in the same jurisdiction in substantially similar cases—became firmly entrenched during this period, contributing further to the establishment of a predictable legal order.

The judges of Massachusetts pioneered in establishing a body of American precedents. Theophilus Parsons, Chief Justice of the Massachusetts Supreme Court from 1806 to 1813, became known as "The Giant of the Law." "He was," says Daniel Boorstin, "a true New Englander both in his feeling for local customs and in his desire, especially in the laws of commerce, shipping, and insurance, to follow the practice of merchants."[4] Lemuel Shaw, Massachusetts Chief Justice from 1830 to 1860, contributed monumentally to the body of common law. He did much to make the law consistent with economic progress by adapting liability provisions to the special circumstances of railroad transportation. He also introduced the notion of "eminent domain," which allowed the *fully compensated* confiscation of private property for public use—as, for example, in establishing a railroad right-of-way. The distinguishing feature of this new legal device was that governments might delegate their confiscatory power to private parties, such as railroad companies, for well-defined and limited purposes. Without the power of eminent domain, it is doubtful that the nation's transportation system, with all its associated social benefits, could have developed as fast as it did.

Law writers also performed a crucial function in the early nineteenth century, for until the existing rules had been systematized, it was difficult

[4] Daniel J. Boorstin, *The Americans: The National Experience* (New York: Random House, 1965), p. 39.

and costly to know the legal consequences of many actions. Though lawyers and judges commonly cited English precedents, some states attempted to restrict their citation, and they were not uniformly observed. As Boorstin properly notes, "Without a general American legal system, technically defined and available in books, the free commerce among our states and the industrial unity of our nation might have been impossible."[5] After the first quarter of the nineteenth century this gap was steadily filled. Landmark writings included Nathan Dane's *General Abridgement and Digest of American Law* (8 vols., 1823), James Kent's *Commentaries on American Law* (4 vols., 1826–30), and the voluminous works of Joseph Story, an Associate Justice of the U. S. Supreme Court, including *Commentaries on the Conflict of Laws* (1834) and *On Equity Jurisprudence* (2 vols., 1836). Among his many accomplishments Story contributed a great deal to the law of patents. All these writers relied on the transcripts of court proceedings prepared by official reporters, appointed first to report United States Supreme Court cases early in the nineteenth century. By the Civil War all the states had official reporters, greatly facilitating the systematic compilation of cases on which the development of common law crucially depends.

From his position as Chief Justice of the U. S. Supreme Court, John Marshall exerted a powerful influence on the establishment of a legal order of security for private property. His long tenure on the court extended from 1801 to 1835, a crucial period in the shaping of American law. Marshall's opinions in the cases of *Fletcher v. Peck* (1810) and *Trustees of Dartmouth College v. Woodward* (1819) were giant steps forward in guaranteeing the sanctity of contracts. In the former case he asked rhetorically: "It may well be doubted whether the nature of society and of the government does not prescribe some limits to the legislative power; and if any be prescribed, where are they to be found, if the property of an individual fairly and honestly acquired, may be seized without compensation?" The Constitution's Contract Clause, he added in the latter case, "must be understood as intended to guard against a power of at least doubtful utility, the abuse of which had been extensively felt, and to restrain the legislature in future from violating the right to property." In *Gibbons v. Ogden* (1824) Marshall declared the validity of the Interstate Commerce Clause in giving the power to regulate interstate trade solely to the federal government, and by proscribing the obstructive actions of individual states he helped to create the legal conditions that would permit the emergence of a broad national market. In all his decisions he was at pains to combat those who would interpret the Con-

[5] *Ibid.*, p. 38.

stitution narrowly, who would "explain away the constitution of our country and leave it a magnificent structure indeed, to look at, but totally unfit for use."[6] In his hands the Constitution became the basic institutional foundation for the promotion of material progress in America's market economy.

As the economy's total output grew in response to the foreign demand for American staples, many inventions became attractive investments for the first time; the acquisition of many skills became worthwhile for the first time; many investments in material capital were justified for the first time. In a setting where property rights were defined and enforced in a way that encouraged invention and protected private property, economic growth could begin. And once under way, the whole process became *self-sustaining*, because material, human, and intellectual capital accumulation led to the growth of output per capita, thus expanding markets and making it worthwhile to invent further, to acquire additional skills, and to accumulate more material capital. In brief, the great transformation that permitted men for the first time to escape from poverty rested on two fundamental bases: (1) the growth of markets, which in the United States had its origins in increasing foreign demand and in population growth under conditions of unlimited land; and (2) the evolution of secure private property rights, including the private right to intellectual property. These developments, stretching back for centuries, have no precise dates of origin. But the Constitution was a major landmark, and in the first half of the nineteenth century, when private property rights became firmly established, several convergent influences finally culminated. By the post-Civil War era, self-sustaining growth had become the normal condition of the American economy.

Of course, nothing guaranteed the continuation of these conditions. But in fact the rights of private property were consolidated and extended during the half century after the Civil War at the same time that markets were growing at unprecedented rates. In the words of the legal historian, Willard Hurst,

> [T]he development of the market steadily increased the interlocking character of operations in this society and thus tended to raise men's need to be able to rely on one another's performance. Various features of our growing law of agreements reflected this. In more and more instances, from mid-century on, the law itself provided a framework for the parties' dealing, unless they explicitly contracted out of the transaction which the rules of law shaped for them. This was notably true in respect to the instruments of commerce—bills of lading, warehouse receipts, stock transfer

[6] *Gibbons v. Ogden* (1824), reprinted in Commager, *op. cit.*, pp. 238–42.

documents—and the forms of association, especially the partnership or corporation.[7]

The culmination of all these developments came when the Supreme Court in the 1880's declared that corporations were legal "persons," extending to them the protection of the Fourteenth Amendment and making it impossible for states to levy discriminatory taxes upon them.

In 1890 the Supreme Court extended the definition of property from physical things to the expected earning power of things—a definition always observed in the market—thereby striking down the power of state legislatures to destroy the value of private property by fixing unreasonably low prices on the services provided by railways and other utilities. A few years later it recognized that earning power depends on free access to markets. In *Allgeyer v. Louisiana* (1897), the court said:

> The liberty mentioned in that Amendment [Fourteenth] means not only the right of the citizen to be free from physical restraint of his person, but the term is deemed to embrace the right of the citizen to be free in the enjoyment of all his faculties; to be free to use them in all lawful ways; to live and work where he will; to earn his livelihood by any lawful calling; to pursue any livelihood or avocation, and for that purpose to enter into all contracts which may be proper, necessary, and essential to his carrying out to a successful conclusion the purposes above mentioned. . . . His enjoyment upon terms of equality with all others in similar circumstances of the privilege of pursuing an ordinary calling or trade, and of acquiring, holding, and selling property is an essential part of liberty and property as guaranteed by the Fourteenth Amendment.[8]

"Institutions," Arthur Lewis has written, "promote or restrict growth according to the protection they accord to effort, according to the opportunities they provide for specialization, and according to the freedom of manoeuvre they permit."[9] In all these respects American institutions were basic to the initiation of economic growth and to its sustainment.

[7] James Willard Hurst, *Law and the Conditions of Freedom in the Nineteenth-Century United States* (Madison, Wis.: University of Wisconsin, 1956), p. 14.

[8] Cited in John R. Commons, *Legal Foundations of Capitalism* (New York: Macmillan, 1924), p. 17. See also pp. 11–16.

[9] W. Arthur Lewis, *The Theory of Economic Growth* (New York: Harper Torchbooks, 1970), p. 57.

III

THE RISE OF CITIES

We had several cities of half a million, and one of more than a million; we had a score of them with a population of a hundred thousand or more. We were very proud of them, and vaunted them as a proof of our unparalleled prosperity, though really they never were anything but congeries of millionaires and the wretched creatures who served them and supplied them. . . . [T]hey were not fit dwelling-places for men, either in the complicated and luxurious palaces where the rich fenced themselves from their kind, or in the vast tenements, towering height upon height, ten and twelve stories up, where the swarming poor festered in vice and sickness and famine.

WILLIAM DEAN HOWELLS

[O]nly the poorest [servants], who cannot find employment in the city, will come to the country, and these as soon as they have got a few dollars ahead, are crazy to get back to town.

FREDERICK LAW OLMSTED

THE URBAN TRANSFORMATION

The most significant aspect of America's transformation in the post-Civil War era was the relative shift of population from the countryside into cities of increasing average size (Table 3.1). At the end of the Civil War, fewer than a quarter of Americans were urban dwellers; 50 years later half the population lived in cities (incorporated places of at least 2500). In 1870 only 14 cities had more than 100,000 inhabitants, but by 1910, 49 places had attained this size, and three—New York, Chicago,

TABLE 3.1
PERCENTAGE OF TOTAL POPULATION URBAN
AND NUMBER OF CITIES

Year	Percentage of Total Population Urban (1)	Number of Cities Over 2500 (2)	Over 100,000 (3)
1870	26	663	14
1880	28	939	20
1890	35	1348	28
1900	40	1737	38
1910	46	2262	49

SOURCE. Col. 1: *United States Census, 1950*: Vol. I, *Population*, p. 1–17. "Urban" means residing within an incorporated place of at least 2500. Cols. 2 and 3: U. S. Bureau of the Census, *Historical Statistics of the United States, Colonial Times to 1957* (Washington: Government Printing Office, 1960), p. 14.

and Philadelphia—exceeded 1.5 million. Indeed, on the eve of the Great War, the population of New York City alone numbered about 5 million! America had become urban as well as industrial, and the consequences were legion.

The urban economy cannot be divorced from the rural economy. Unless the productivity of agricultural workers somewhere in the world is high enough to support both the farmers' families and a substantial number of others, no large city can exist. Given a sufficiently high level of agricultural productivity to support cities, they might exist for a variety of reasons, some of a noneconomic nature. The first known cities, founded several thousand years ago, apparently served as centers of political administration and religious observance; some modern cities—Washington, D. C., for example—also rest on such a basis. Modern cities, however, are generally *economic* entities, and only by considering them as such can we understand their growth during the past two centuries. Urbanization, a steady increase in the urban population relative to the total population, required that agricultural productivity be continually rising; in effect, it required economic growth. This relation explains why, even as late as 1800, the bulk of the population everywhere was rural, and large cities were a great rarity. But if urbanization was a consequence of economic growth, it was also a cause, for cities served in various ways to accelerate the rate of productivity increase. (Some of these urban contributions to economic growth we shall discuss later in this chapter.)

An illuminating way to understand cities as economic entities is by constructing a theory that implies that no cities would exist! Since cities do exist, we know that one or more of the assumptions of such a theory must be false. But therein lies the purpose of the exercise, for the negations of these assumptions provide sufficient reasons for the existence of cities. Such a "no-cities model" helps to clarify our thinking about the economic bases of cities.[1]

The no-cities model contains three assumptions. First, suppose that the earth is a featureless plain, having everywhere the same topography, climate, fertility, and mineral content. Next, suppose that all economic activities are characterized by constant cost; that is, no matter how much output were produced, the average cost of producing a single unit would be the same. Finally, assume that all markets, whether for outputs or inputs, are perfectly competitive. From these assumptions it follows logically that no city will exist, for a concentration of population entails no economic advantage but has a definite disadvantage. The assumptions imply that every consumer can produce the bundle of goods he desires at the site where he wishes to consume it with no loss of efficiency—average cost and output level are independent, and resources are ubiquitous—at the same time avoiding all transportation costs. Furthermore, the population under these conditions will spread itself out at the minimum possible density, because any attempt at agglomeration would raise land rents without any compensating benefit.

The prediction of the no-cities model obviously fails to correspond with reality, and the reasons are plain. First, the earth is far from homogeneous. Areas differ widely in topography, climate, fertility, mineral content, accessibility, and other features. It may therefore prove advantageous to concentrate production in a small area—around a mineral deposit or at a river or railroad junction—forming a city even though the production of commodities occurs at constant cost. Generally, however, we cannot maintain the constant-cost assumption. Especially at rather small output levels, it seems characteristic of many production processes that average unit cost declines as the rate of output increases; that is, economies of scale exist. Concentration of production may then occur because the resulting reductions in average cost more than compensate for the expenses of transportation incurred in assembling raw materials and distributing the finished product to dispersed customers. In sum, cities can exist because of natural or man-made heterogeneity in the spatial environment and because of economies of scale.

Once a city exists, locating there allows savings of transportation

[1] The first exposition of the no-cities model appears in Tjalling C. Koopmans, *Three Essays on the State of Economic Science* (New York: McGraw-Hill, 1957), pp. 153–54; see also Edwin S. Mills, "An Aggregative Model of Resource Allocation in a Metropolitan Area," *American Economic Review*, LVII (May 1967), 198.

costs for many businesses that serve the local market. The city may also attract new businesses because the presence of already established activities reduces the costs of operating related businesses or because larger cities can more efficiently supply certain municipal services like police and fire protection, good streets, water, and power. Because such advantages of an urban location do not depend on the actions of any individual firm, economists describe them as "external economies" from the point of view of the firm. New and expanded businesses in turn attract new workers. Of course, at some point firms in a growing city begin to encounter external *dis*economies in the form of traffic and housing congestion, environmental pollution, and overloaded municipal facilities of all kinds. In this case the growth of the city imposes costs on the firm that are independent of the firm's own actions. Whether a city will attract new businesses and migrants therefore depends in part on the balance between external economies and diseconomies as well as on the potential newcomers' knowledge of these things, which is always imperfect.

We have already seen that economic growth gives rise to changes, especially in expenditure patterns, that encourage the movement of resources out of agriculture and into manufacturing, trade, transportation, and other nonagricultural activities. By itself this need not lead to the growth of urban population, for nonagricultural goods might conceivably be produced in the countryside. But in fact, these kinds of production typically appear in an urban setting. One reason is that while farming is generally a constant-cost industry, many nonagricultural activities are subject to economies of scale. In addition, these activities often benefit from the external economies realizable only in cities. In short, they are most remunerative when conducted on a large scale—which itself may create a city—or when located in already existing cities. With rising incomes, demand rose relatively faster for nonagricultural goods, and therefore aggregate production increasingly concentrated in urban areas. The result was a more rapid growth of urban than of total population.

This argument explains why the urban population became relatively larger, but it does not explain how urban population gains were divided between an enlargement of existing cities and the establishment of new cities. To answer this question we must distinguish between at least two kinds of city: one is commercial, producing mostly services, and the other has a substantial concentration of manufacturing along with its service activities.

For statistical purposes we shall follow the Census Bureau in defining a city as an incorporated place of at least 2500 people. In the post-Civil War era most cities engaged primarily in commercial functions, especially in retail trade, and only a minority possessed substantial amounts

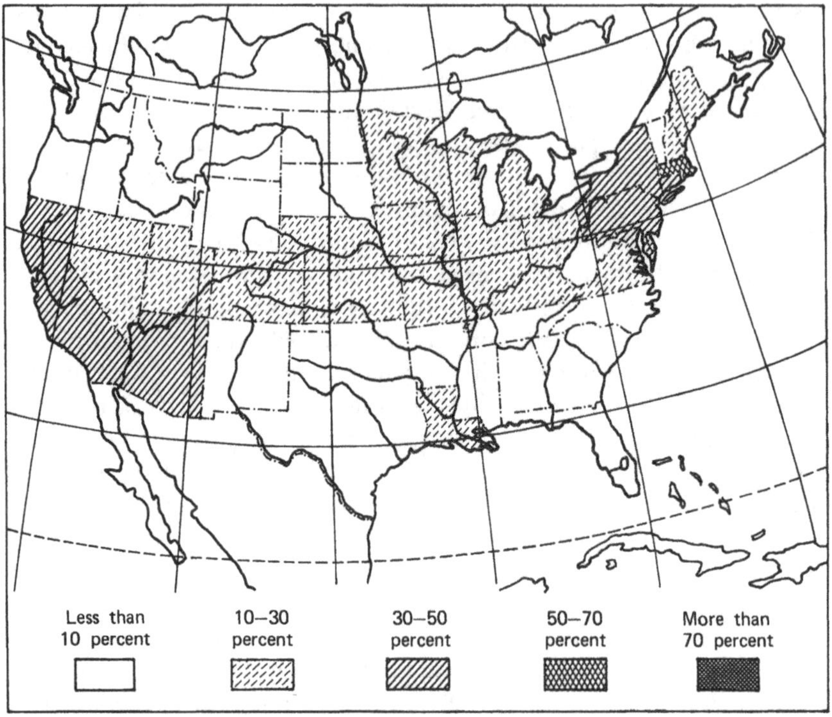

Figure 3.1 Percentage urban in 1870, by states. *Source: United States Census, 1950:* Vol. I, *Population,* pp. 1–17 to 1–23.

of manufacturing. This pattern prevailed everywhere, but it was particularly evident in the South and the West, where very few cities belonged to the manufacturing category. Most of the manufacturing cities appeared in the Northeast and Great Lakes regions. As the population became more densely settled and per capita incomes rose, more and more commercial cities—geographers aptly describe them as "central places"—grew up in the East. And in the West agricultural settlement and the establishment of central places went hand in hand. The South, with lower incomes and less active trade, witnessed less of this kind of urbanization, but even there the same process occurred (Figures 3.1 and 3.2). In every case the reasons were the same. Farmers and other rural people demanded food, clothing, lumber, fuel, and blacksmith's services at frequent intervals, and it was uneconomical for them to travel very far to make such purchases. Providing such goods, as well as a railroad station and local markets and storage facilities for farm products, was the function of the central places of 2500 to 10,000 people. Such places linked a large rural

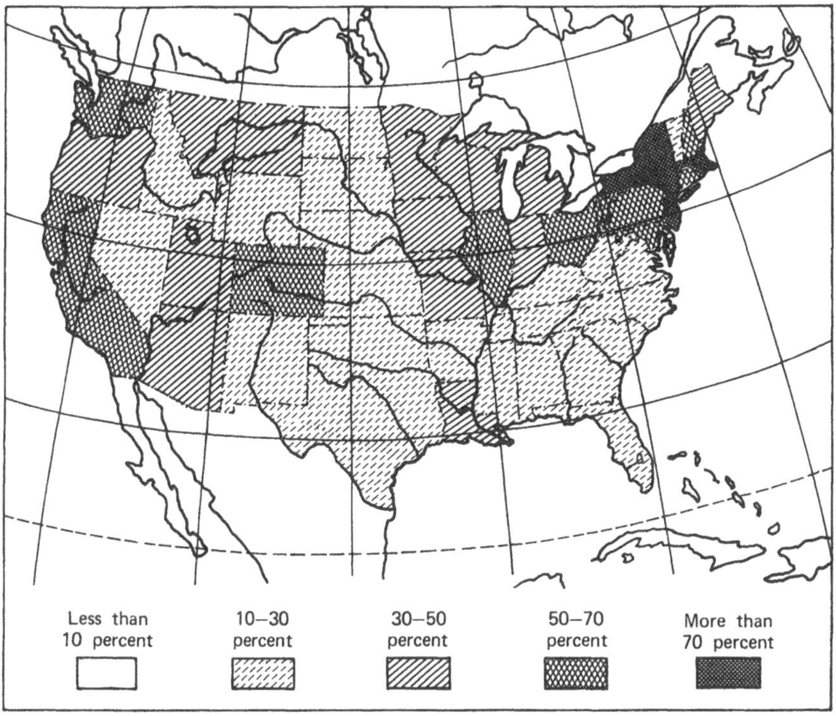

Figure 3.2 Percentage urban in 1910, by states. *Source: United States Census, 1950:* Vol. I, *Population,* pp. 1–17 to 1–23.

population to the rest of the economy, thereby promoting greater specialization. Commercial agriculture like that in the American West could operate efficiently only with the aid of hundreds of almost uniformly scattered central place cities. Significantly, in 1870 almost 500 of America's 663 cities had populations of less than 10,000; and forty years later 1665 of 2262 cities were in this size class. Of course, not all these small cities were central places. Some exploited minerals; others, particularly in the Far West, provided mainly transportation services; and a few, especially in New England, attracted manufacturing enterprises. But most cities of 2500 to 10,000 were occupied in facilitating the exchange of manufactured goods and urban services for farm products. In brief, the vast majority of America's cities served central place functions, and the expansion in the number of such places depended quite simply on the increasing rural population density and the rising level of per capita income. As long as local transportation was by horse and wagon these small cities would continue to thrive. We must not forget that the rural population, although declining in relative terms, grew in absolute terms, from less than 27 million in 1870 to about 50 million in 1910. This rural population also became more and more specialized, demanding more and more urban-supplied goods. A rapid expansion in the number of central place cities was a predictable consequence.[2]

Central place theory allows us to explain the growth of the great majority of American cities in the post-Civil War era. Places of 2500 to 10,000 accounted for only a fraction—declining from 24 percent in 1870 to 19 percent in 1910—of the total urban population, but many larger cities also served central place functions; indeed, a complete theory of central places predicts that a regular hierarchy of such cities will emerge. Small central place cities exist because their businesses can supply some services so cheaply, on a relatively large scale, that people in the surrounding countryside will incur transportation costs in obtaining such services from the city and still be better off than if they provided them for themselves. But while small-city businesses can realize a normal rate of return on the production of some services, the city faces too small a demand to support a full range of potential urban economic activities. We do not expect to find a stockbroker, a symphony orchestra, or a brain surgeon in a town of 2500. The residents of small towns must obtain such services in larger cities, where the demand is sufficient to support them. Because a continuum of such "demand thresholds" exists, the larger a city is, the greater is the variety of businesses it will contain. The city of 50,000 can surely boast a stockbroker, but the symphony appears only in larger places. Small cities contain businesses whose economies of scale exist only at relatively small output levels; larger cities support businesses whose economies of scale continue relatively longer as output expands. The larger the city, the greater is its "range," the maximum distance from which its customers travel. Greater scale economies, and hence lower costs and prices, justify the buyer's incurring greater transportation costs. And the larger the city, the smaller is the proportion of its customers from rural areas, for very large cities serve many buyers and sellers from smaller cities as well as people from the nearby countryside. Larger central place cities prominent in the post-Civil War era included such places as Atlanta, Indianapolis, Des Moines, Sacramento, and Spokane. And surrounding each of these cities was a hierarchy of smaller places, often following a fairly regular rule that the second-ranking place was about one half as large as the largest, the third-ranking place about one third as large as the largest, and so forth.

[2] For some statistical tests of hypotheses derived from central place theory, see Robert Higgs, "The Growth of Cities in a Midwestern Region, 1870–1900," *Journal of Regional Science*, IX (Dec. 1969).

The appearance of such hierarchies confirmed that the free market provided an efficient spatial allocation of activities and resources.[3]

In 1870 the 14 cities of 100,000 or more contained over 4 million people, more than 40 percent of the total urban population; in 1910 the 49 cities of this size class housed more than 20 million, almost half of the vastly enlarged urban population. Here we find the urban America that stirred the strongest emotions among reformers and rural boosters: the great monster New York, with its towering skyscrapers and cramped tenements; sprawling Chicago,

> Hog Butcher for the World,
> Tool Maker, Stacker of Wheat,
> Player with Railroads and the Nation's Freight Handler;
> Stormy, husky, brawling,
> City of the Big Shoulders.[4]

Here also are dingy Philadelphia, tubercular Boston, and noisome Baltimore that reminded H. L. Mencken of "a billion polecats." Table 3.2 shows how dramatically the great American cities expanded in the half century before 1910.

Within these cities lay the bulk of the nation's manufacturing. In 1890, ten major cities—all those in Table 3.2 except Los Angeles—accounted for almost 40 percent of the value added in American manufacturing. Indeed, some cities were commonly identified with their major manufacturing industry: Pittsburgh with iron and steel; Kansas City and Omaha with meat-packing; Minneapolis with flour milling; Detroit, just before World War I, with automobiles. The great cities were also the focus of commerce, finance, and communications. In general, the larger the city, the greater was the number of distinct industries represented there. Though the largest cities almost without exception contained extensive manufacturing activities, they were at the same time more diversified than smaller urban places, as central place theory would predict.

But central place theory applies to mainly commercial cities; it is inadequate to explain the growth of the great manufacturing centers. We must explain the awesome expansion of these cities primarily as a result of the attempt by businessmen to benefit from the external economies inherent in urban agglomeration. The printing and publishing trades provide a good illustration. These businesses were typically located near

3 On the development of urban hierarchies, see Harvey S. Perloff, *et al.*, *Regions, Resources, and Economic Growth* (Baltimore: Johns Hopkins, 1960), pp. 17–19; and Robert Higgs, "Central Place Theory and Regional Urban Hierarchies: An Empirical Note," *Journal of Regional Science*, X (Aug. 1970).

4 Carl Sandburg, "Chicago," 1916.

TABLE 3.2

POPULATIONS OF ELEVEN LARGE CITIES, 1860 AND 1910

City	City Population 1860 (Thousands)	City Population 1910 (Thousands)	Metropolitan District Population 1910 (Thousands)
New York	1175	4767	6475
Chicago	112	2185	2447
Philadelphia	566	1549	1972
Boston	178	671	1520
Pittsburgh	49	534	1045
St. Louis	161	687	829
San Francisco	57	417	687
Baltimore	212	558	659
Cleveland	43	561	613
Detroit	46	466	501
Los Angeles	4	319	438

SOURCE. Allan R. Pred, *The Spatial Dynamics of U. S. Urban-Industrial Growth, 1800–1914* (Cambridge, Mass.: M. I. T. Press, 1966), p. 23.

the city center. Because they depended on a great deal of face-to-face negotiation between buyers and sellers—economists have described them as "communications oriented"—it was essential that they occupy a location of maximum accessibility within the city. In a large city a variety of specialized printing and publishing trades could flourish, and the accessibility and efficiency of these specialized producers accrued as an external economy to their customers within the city. In a host of other cases the concentrated market represented by a great city encouraged the emergence of specialized producers whose enhanced efficiency became an external economy from their customers' point of view. As noted above, municipal utilities subject to economies of scale, such as electrical power generation, also provided external economies to the businesses in large cities.

The dense press of population and economic activity on limited urban land areas pushed land rents to astronomical levels. In the absence of complete data on rents, information on land values provides a good substitute. In Chicago's central business district, the square mile surrounding State and Madison streets, for example, the value of the land increased during 1873–1910 from about $72 million to about $600 million, an amazing increase of over 700 percent. In 1910 this small area accounted for 40 percent of the value of *all* the land in Chicago![5] That businessmen valued the land so highly is clear testimony to the advantages of a central location in a great city.

We can now summarize our discussion of the urban transformation. The reasons for the rise in the urban proportion of the population lay in two forces: the economic growth that gave rise to changing expenditure patterns increasingly emphasizing nonagricultural goods, and the decreasing-cost and external-economies characteristics of the activities by which these goods were produced. Under these conditions it was advantageous for entrepreneurs increasingly to concentrate their production in cities. In the process the number of cities grew, mainly by a proliferation of central places attributable to rising per capita income and population density in the rural areas. Although this kind of urban expansion occurred in all regions, it can be seen most clearly in the West, where agricultural settlement and the establishment of hundreds of new central places occurred concomitantly. The enormous growth of the largest cities had its sources in the attempt by businessmen to realize the economies inherent in urban agglomeration and at the same time in many cases to save transportation costs while serving a large local market.

THE ECONOMICS OF IMPROVING URBAN HEALTH

Rapid urbanization raised many new health problems and exacerbated some old ones. In an era when highly communicable, infectious diseases were responsible for most deaths and a great deal of sickness, agglomeration of the population in densely inhabited areas had obvious drawbacks. The primitive state of medical and public health knowledge militated against an effective approach to solving these problems in the immediate post-Civil War years, but the emergence of bacteriology largely eliminated this critical obstacle; by 1890 the germ theory was widely known and accepted. In the three decades before America's entry into the Great War the health improvements realized, though often dependent on the progress of scientific knowledge, were largely the outcome of *economic* decisions. The investments made by urban people in an attempt to reap the returns of improved health were important in their own right, but

[5] Homer Hoyt, *One Hundred Years of Land Values in Chicago* (Chicago: University of Chicago, 1933), p. 337.

in many cases they had an additional dimension: they represented attempts by governments to improve on conditions in which the unhampered action of individuals failed to promote the social welfare.

In the mid-nineteenth century the health of urban dwellers was markedly inferior to that of rural people. While the death rate in the countryside was not much over 20 per 1000 population, the death rate in the large cities was in the neighborhood of 30. The reasons for this wide divergence are apparent. Dense concentration of population increased the likelihood that communicable diseases such as tuberculosis and diphtheria would spread directly from person to person. Water wells were more likely to be fouled by drainage from poorly sealed privies, and alternative forms of water supply were relatively very expensive. Safe sewage disposal was enormously more difficult than in the countryside. Urban people had less access to fresh milk, fruits, and vegetables, and a poor diet made them easy targets for a variety of infectious diseases.

Beginning in the 1880's substantial improvements were made in urban health conditions. In part these gains reflected the rising income levels that allowed people to enjoy better diets and more spacious housing. To some extent, however, they resulted from conscious efforts to improve the public health aspects of the environment. These efforts included the provision of pure water supplies and improved means of sewage disposal, the pasteurization of milk, regular garbage collection, swamp drainage, and a variety of other actions. The results were striking. In a group of 35 large cities in 1898–1908, 17 had a typhoid death rate of more than 30 per 100,000 and the others all had a rate exceeding 15; by 1917–19 all but two of these cities had reduced the rate to less than 15.[6] As Table 3.3 suggests, the reduction in death rates applied as well to all the major infectious diseases.

Individuals often made expenditures for improved health in the free market. One could voluntarily allocate more of his income toward obtaining a better diet or more spacious living quarters, though lack of knowledge about nutrition hampered the former effort. The important point, however, is that within the constraints of their incomes and their knowledge, consumers had full command over the purchase of better health in these ways; the success of one man's investment in improved health did not depend on the actions of his neighbors.

In other cases interdependencies prevented individuals from acting alone successfully. Suppose, for example, that John Doe had discovered the ill effects of privy drainage in contaminating his well. He might then

[6] C.-E. A. Winslow, *The Evolution and Significance of the Modern Public Health Campaign* (New Haven: Yale University, 1923), p. 38.

TABLE 3.3
DEATHS PER 100,000 POPULATION IN NEW YORK, BOSTON, PHILADELPHIA, AND NEW ORLEANS

Disease	Annual Average 1864–88	Annual Average 1889–1913
Tuberculosis	365	223
Stomach and Intestinal	299	196
Scarlet Fever	66	19
Typhoid and Typhus	53	25
Smallpox	40	2
Cholera	8	0
Diphtheria	123	58
Yellow Fever	14	1

SOURCE. Frederick L. Hoffman, "American Mortality Progress During the Last Half Century," in Mazyck P. Ravenel, *A Half Century of Public Health* (New York: American Public Health Association, 1921), p. 102.

have invested in the construction of a properly sealed privy; but it was likely to be a waste of money, because he had no way of compelling his neighbors to undertake similar investments. Unless *everyone* acted together, any individual's efforts were unlikely to be successful.

One way of dealing with such cases is through negotiation and mutual agreement, perhaps including pecuniary compensations, among the parties involved. When the number of involved persons is very large, however, as it typically is in urban public health problems, this kind of negotiated agreement is quite difficult and costly; such problems are therefore seldom resolved in this way.

An alternative manner of approaching these problems is through government action. Because of the government's ability to coerce uncooperative minorities and to assure a minimum of "free riding" by taxing all the beneficiaries of a public investment, government actions have often taken the place of the market in cases where important interdependencies prevent individuals from acting effectively. In dealing with the problems of urban public health this approach was generally successful, even though it opened new avenues for corruption and political conflict. Sanitary regulations enforced by newly created urban health boards, compulsory vaccination against smallpox, tenement building codes, and public investments in water purification and sewage disposal furnish examples of the wide range of government actions undertaken in the field of urban public health during the post-Civil War era.

Water filtration provides a striking illustration. Before the late nineteenth century, people generally judged the quality of water according to its clarity and taste, without regard for the disease-carrying organisms it might harbor. With the development of bacteriology, the public increasingly demanded filters capable of straining out harmful bacteria, and inventors soon developed a variety of such devices. These reduced the incidence of many diseases, especially typhoid. Filtration lowered the typhoid death rate per 100,000 population from 121 to 26 in Lawrence, Massachusetts; from 104 to 26 in Albany, N. Y.; from 49 to 11 in Binghamton, N. Y.; and from 68 to 20 in Watertown, N. Y.[7] Table 3.4 shows

TABLE 3.4

EFFECT OF FILTRATION ON DEATH RATES AT ALBANY, N.Y., AND A COMPARISON WITH TROY, N.Y., WHERE THE WATER WAS NOT FILTERED

	Death Rate per 100,000		Percentage Reduction
	1894–98	1900–1904	
ALBANY			
Typhoid Fever	104	26	75
Diarrheal diseases	125	53	57
Children under 5 years	606	309	49
Total deaths	2264	1868	17
TROY			
Typhoid Fever	57	57	0
Diarrheal diseases	116	102	12
Children under 5 years	513	435	18
Total deaths	2157	2028	6

SOURCE. George C. Whipple, *Typhoid Fever: Its Causation, Transmission and Prevention* (New York: John Wiley and Sons, 1908), p. 276.

by a dramatic contrast how powerful the impact of filtration could be: Albany installed its filter in 1899; Troy's water supply came from the same source, the Hudson River, without filtration.

The interrelated problems of water supply and sewage disposal in Chicago provide another interesting case. Before 1900 the city used Lake Michigan both as a source of water and as a receptacle for sewage. A high incidence of typhoid, including periodic epidemics, was just one of the undesirable consequences. As the city and its sewage discharge continued their spectacular growth, Chicagoans found this arrangement more

[7] George C. Whipple, *Typhoid Fever: Its Causation, Transmission, and Prevention* (New York: John Wiley and Sons, 1908), pp. 281-82.

and more intolerable. The city's low elevation compounded its sewerage problems, natural drainage being almost totally lacking. In 1886 the Chicago City Council created the Drainage and Water Supply Commission, which finally provided a solution by diverting all sewage from Lake Michigan, discharging it into the Des Plaines River, from which it passed into the Illinois River and hence into the Mississippi River drainage system. This scheme also reversed the direction of the Chicago River's flow to provide a flushing action for the sewage discharge. Work on the project began in 1890, but the drainage canal did not open until 1900.

Few cities required as spectacular an effort as Chicago's. Still, the problems were seldom easily solved, and continued urban expansion often made facilities inadequate soon after their installation. On balance, however, public health workers made great progress. Compulsory vaccination, for example, reduced smallpox from a major killer to a statistical rarity by World War I. Filters, chlorination, and aqueducts from pure mountain streams dramatically improved the quality of water supplies. Compulsory pasteurization of milk reduced the incidence of tuberculosis, typhoid, and a variety of other diseases. Construction of modern sewer systems contributed greatly toward a more healthful environment. In the words of a distinguished public health worker, "The two decades between 1890 and 1910 formed in a sense the golden age of public health. . . . No previous period of twenty years had ever seen equal progress in the application of sanitary science and it is doubtful if any similar period in the future will ever witness quite such phenomenal achievements."[8]

Significantly, almost all these improvements involved substantial investments. Contemporaries were well aware of the costs but were convinced that the benefits far exceeded them. Recognizing the greater productivity of healthier workers, the economic losses from deaths, and the waste of resources attending sickness, a sanitary engineer asserted in 1908: "To remedy all these conditions will cost money, but it will pay. It will pay not only in the satisfaction of having clean and healthful cities to live in, not only in the joy of having relieved the suffering and saved the dying, but it will pay in hard cash."[9] Often these investments promised a positive return only when undertaken by governments or under the umbrella of government sponsorship or authority. The interdependencies that made it difficult or impossible for individuals to cope successfully with the problems of urban health did not forever block a solution, for in this area governments proved their capability for pro-

[8] Winslow, *op. cit.*, pp. 36–37.

[9] Whipple, *op. cit.*, p. 285.

viding services where the free market could not function properly. Moreover, a by-product of these government actions was a more rapid dissemination of the new public health knowledge than would otherwise have occurred—for example, through the school nurse program—and with this knowledge people could better act individually to improve their health.

In his recent study of investments in improving health within a group of Northeastern states during the period 1880–1910, Edward F. Meeker considers expenditures made on sanitary sewers, pure water supplies, and municipal health conservation projects. He then estimates the monetary value of increased life expectancy and reductions in work missed because of sickness. The rate of return implied by these costs and benefits is 25 percent. Though Meeker qualifies this result in various ways to take into account unmeasurable costs and benefits, his findings suggest strongly that investments in health paid a substantially greater return than investments in material capital during the late nineteenth and early twentieth centuries.[10]

URBANIZATION AND INVENTION

While urbanization depended on economic growth, the converse was also true, for the concentration of the population in cities increased the rate of advance in productivity. Entrepreneurs employing techniques that were relatively efficient when conducted on a large scale often created cities around their plants; more often they simply located in existing cities, where their labor demands could be readily satisfied. A variety of external economies attracted businessmen to the cities. New ideas spread more rapidly in an urban environment, and hence the average plant became more up-to-date than it would have been under conditions of geographically dispersed production.

Urbanization also stimulated economic growth by facilitating an expanded flow of inventions. Inventive activity, we have previously argued, is generally an economic endeavor; the greater the expected rate of return, the more inventions will be forthcoming. By extending this argument to include a spatial dimension, we can show that urban people would be expected to produce more inventions than rural people.

An invention is usefully defined as a new combination of previously

[10] Edward F. Meeker, *The Economics of Improving Health, 1850–1915* (Unpublished doctoral dissertation, University of Washington, 1970), pp. 117–53.

existing knowledge that satisfies some want. Inventive activity, then, is nothing more than the process of creating new useful information. From this conception of inventive activity, it is only a short step to postulating that just two inputs enter the process: inventive talent and prior information.

If we suppose that inventive talent (native creativity) is distributed throughout the population independently of location, then differences in inventive activity among regions or places must depend on variations in the expected costs of acquiring information. Since rates of return depend on both revenues and costs, two kinds of information are relevant. The first is information about opportunities for invention, that is, about the extent of the market for invention; the second is information that can serve as inputs into the production of inventions. The former determines the potential inventor's expectation of the revenue stream that his invention will generate, while the latter determines his expectation of the cost of producing the invention. Together these imply an expected rate of return, a signal encouraging him either to devote his energies to inventive activity or to use his talents and time in an alternative manner. To link inventiveness to urbanization within this analytical framework, we must show that information costs differed systematically between rural and urban areas. Such differences are in fact quite plausible for the post-Civil War era.

The expected rate of return depends in part on the expected stream of revenue from invention. Under conditions preceding mass communication, when most reliable information was acquired by direct observation or by word of mouth, the average search cost of information about potential markets for inventions was an increasing function of market distance; therefore, the market *as perceived by a potential inventor* was largely restricted to nearby locations. Assuming that the locational distribution of actual inventive opportunities coincided with that of the population, the probability that an opportunity would be perceived was then much higher for urban than for rural persons. Given the assumed relation between market distance and the average search cost of information, this proposition follows from the common definition of a city as an area of spatially agglomerated population. Moreover, if the more reasonable assumption is made that, in relation to population, actual inventive opportunities were disproportionately concentrated in the cities, there are even stronger grounds for postulating that the expected stream of revenue from invention was larger for urban than for rural persons.

The expected rate of return also depends on the expected costs of inventing, and here we propose an inverse relation with urbanization. "In a pre-mass-communications context, such as the relatively compact cities of the late nineteenth century, where diffusion of technical knowledge [was] highly reliant upon personal interaction, the possibilities for invention ought to [have been] enhanced by the . . . network of interpersonal communications and confrontations."[11] In the absence of well-developed means of mass communication, the costs of acquiring information depended heavily on *spatial proximity*. The expected search costs of acquiring informational inputs were lower for the potential urban inventor than for his rural counterpart simply because of the enormously greater proximity of urban information carriers to one another. The greatest handicap of rural persons was their spatial isolation from one another. To the extent that urban people were better educated, their advantages were compounded.

Combining the assumptions about the expected revenue stream and the expected total costs of inventing, we conclude that the expected rate of return on inventive activity was higher in the city than in the countryside. It is now easy to derive the testable hypothesis that, other things being equal, an increasing linear relation existed between inventiveness—that is, inventions *per capita*—and the proportion of the population in cities.[12]

A substantial body of evidence is consistent with this view of inventiveness. One recent study found that among American states in the 1870–1920 period a difference of 10 percentage points in the proportion of the population living in cities was positively associated with a difference of 6–9 patents per 100,000 population, even when the influences of manufacturing and regional differences were held constant.[13] Another study found that within Connecticut, the nation's most inventive state, urbanization and inventiveness were closely associated. Citizens of the 12 largest cities generally provided about three fourths of all the patented inventions in a large random sample, and the number of inventions *per*

[11] Allan R. Pred, *The Spatial Dynamics of U. S. Urban-Industrial Growth, 1800–1914* (Cambridge, Mass.: M. I. T. Press, 1966), p. 96.

[12] This proof requires only a little algebra. By definition, the total number of inventions I is the sum of those made by urban people Iu and those made by rural people Ir. Thus, $I = Iu + Ir$. Iu is proportional to the urban population Pu, and Ir is proportional to the rural population Pr; but because of differences in the search costs of information, and therefore in the expected rate of return on inventive activity, the urban proportionality factor α is greater than the rural proportionality factor β. Thus, $Iu = \alpha Pu$, and $Ir = \beta Pr$, where $\alpha > \beta > 0$. If we substitute these equations into the definition of I and divide both sides of the equation by the total population P, we obtain an expression for inventiveness: $I/P = \alpha Pu/P + \beta Pr/P$. Since $Pr/P = (1 - Pu/P)$, it follows that $I/P = \beta + (\alpha - \beta) Pu/P$, where $(\alpha - \beta) > 0$.

[13] Robert Higgs, "American Inventiveness, 1870–1920," *Journal of Political Economy*, LXXIX (May/June 1971).

TABLE 3.5
ESTIMATED LEVELS OF PATENTED INVENTIONS PER 10,000 POPULATION, CONNECTICUT LOCATIONS, 1870–1910

	1870	1880	1890	1900	1910
Group I					
Bridgeport	21.6	26.1	20.2	18.7	11.8
Hartford	11.8	7.1	24.8	19.0	19.7
New Haven	24.0	18.3	12.7	10.9	10.1
Waterbury	24.1	25.3	40.9	4.1	6.8
Meriden	39.0	21.3	30.4	9.5	11.0
New Britain	11.6	22.9	68.5	7.3	30.8
Group I Aggregate	17.7	18.1	25.2	13.1	13.9
Group II					
New London	7.3	5.7	6.5	2.3	5.1
Stamford	70.0	60.0	30.2	40.6	17.9
Middletown	21.7	22.1	31.1	11.5	21.0
Norwich	22.2	9.9	17.3	2.3	0.0
Danbury	12.5	2.6	19.9	4.8	9.9
Norwalk	13.9	0.0	27.7	18.1	6.3
Group II Aggregate	17.3	9.7	20.1	12.8	9.7
Groups I and II Aggregate	17.6	16.1	24.1	13.0	13.1
Group III (All other locations)	11.7	6.0	3.8	3.8	4.1

SOURCE. Robert Higgs, "Cities and Yankee Ingenuity, 1870–1920," in Kenneth T. Jackson and Stanley Schultz, Eds., *From Village to Metropolis: Essays on the City in America* (New York: Knopf, 1972).

capita was generally more than twice as great in these cities as elsewhere in the state (Table 3.5).

These findings may well be significant for the explanation of economic growth as a *self-sustaining* process during the post-Civil War era. To vastly oversimplify, urbanization was a response to changes in the relative rates of return on agricultural and nonagricultural activities, which in turn resulted largely from changes in expenditure patterns as per capita incomes rose. In brief, economic growth gave rise to urbanization. But because urbanization encouraged greater inventiveness, it produced a *feedback effect* on growth by promoting more rapid technological progress. In this way urbanization was a cause as well as a consequence of economic growth, and the circle of a self-sustaining process was closed. Even if the existence of this feedback mechanism is granted, however, the magnitude of its influence on growth remains open to conjecture.

CITY VERSUS COUNTRY: THE NATURE OF THE CHOICE

In the post-Civil War era rapid urbanization gave rise to a variety of problems. Housing, sanitation, water, education, and many other goods were demanded on an unprecedented scale, and supplies expanded only after a lag. Slums, with their associated crime and disease, developed at a frightening pace in the larger cities, inspiring a whole generation of reformers toward projects of civic improvement. But no matter how loudly critics might damn the process of urbanization, urban businesses boomed and the migration to the cities continued unabated. Rural virtues were still extolled, but by their actions both Americans and immigrants revealed that the city, even with all its defects and problems, seemed preferable to the countryside.

Unfamiliar with and romantic about rural life, many modern scholars have regarded this migration as rather paradoxical, as a movement from bad to worse. Contemporary writers and later historians alike have heavily emphasized the unsavory aspects of urbanization; slum housing, unemployment, disease, crime, and alienation figure prominently in urban histories and collections of documents. A California farmer in 1884 declared it "inexplicable that the charms of the city should be sufficiently potential [sic] to attract the boys and girls from the firesides of the country."[14] Perhaps the question should be raised: was the movement to the cities a great mistake? After all, people do make mistakes, and it is easy to believe that many migrated to the city expecting something that was not really there. Nevertheless, this is a weak interpretation, for it seems highly unlikely that a movement based on false information would have continued unabated over more than a century. Though people sometimes make mistakes, they also learn from experience and attempt to rectify their mistakes.

Without ignoring the problems of the city, it is possible to interpret the migration as a rational response to alternative opportunities. Henry

[14] A. G. Burnett, "Address to California State Agricultural Society," *Transactions of the California State Agricultural Society during the Year 1884* (Sacramento, 1885), reprinted in *Agricultural History*, XLII (April 1968), 102.

George's characterization was surely close to the situation as perceived by millions of common rural people:

> Consider the barrenness of the isolated farmer's life—the dull round of work and sleep, in which so much of it passes. Consider, what is still worse, the monotonous existence to which his wife is condemned; its lack of recreation and excitement, and of gratifications of taste, and of the sense of harmony and beauty; its steady drag of cares and toils that make women worn and wrinkled when they should be in their bloom. Even the discomforts and evils of the crowded tenement-house are not worse than the discomforts and evils of such a life.[15]

Even the farmer quoted earlier, who found the movement to the cities puzzling, admitted at another point that "farm life is too often the synonym for unrequited toil and harrowing discontent."[16] (In the next chapter we shall elaborate on these observations of rural life.)

A more important point, however, is that focusing on urban *problems* gives a distorted view of city life. Only a minority of city dwellers lived in the festering slums, yet the stories of these people make up a major portion of the literature of urban social and economic history. At the very least the higher money incomes earned by urban people should be noted. In 1890, for example, estimated average annual earnings were $233 for farm laborers; they were $439 for manufacturing workers, the bulk of whom lived in cities.[17] No doubt some of this difference can be attributed to the greater skills of the average manufacturing worker and to the lower costs of living in the countryside, but it is probable that even after such corrections a substantial gap would remain. Income differences, however, were but one aspect of the advantages of urban living. The range of commodities and services on which the higher urban incomes might be spent was enormously greater than in the countryside. Cultural amenities like the theater and concert music were available only in cities. The libraries were there; so were the daily newspapers—not to mention telephones and electric lights. Sociologists have said a great deal about urban alienation, yet from the perspective of the former resident of an isolated farmstead, the mere proximity of neighbors opened up new opportunities for social intercourse, if nothing more than a drink and conversation after work.

The accounts of contemporary writers, reformers, and social workers

[15] Henry George, *The Writings of Henry George* (New York: Doubleday and McClure, 1898), III, 236.

[16] Burnett, *op. cit.*, 102.

[17] U. S. Bureau of the Census, *Historical Statistics of the United States, Colonial Times to 1957* (Washington: Government Printing Office, 1960), p. 92.

can be highly misleading. Ultimately people reveal their preferences by their actual choices, and in the post-Civil War era they increasingly chose an urban residence. We can surely learn a good deal about the cities—and the countryside—by focusing on the reasons for that choice, by considering it not as a paradox but as a rational response to alternative opportunities. The problems of urbanization ought to be recognized, but our calculations must include benefits as well as costs if we are to assess the welfare effects of the movement to the cities.

IV

THE UPS AND DOWNS OF THE FARMER

This is a new age to the farmer. He is now, more than ever before, a citizen of the world. Cheap and excellent books and periodical publications load the shelf and the table in his sitting room and parlor. He travels more than he ever did before, and he travels longer distances. His children are receiving a better education than he received himself, and they dress better than he did when he was a child. They are more frequently in contact with town and city life than he was. They have a top buggy, and a fancy whip, and a pretty lap robe, with a fast stepping horse, whereas their father had an old wagon and a less expensive horse. The farmer's table is better too; his food is more varied, and more of it is bought by him and less of it is raised on his farm.

George K. Holmes

[N]o splendor of cloud, no grace of sunset could conceal the poverty of these people, on the contrary they brought out, with a more intolerable poignancy, the gracelessness of these homes, and the sordid quality of the mechanical routine of these lives.

Hamlin Garland

AGRICULTURAL DEVELOPMENT

The development of American agriculture in the half century after the Civil War was so complex—not to say perplexing—that no simple description is possible. In some ways this period was a veritable Golden Age of agriculture; in other ways, it was, at least until the late 1890's, a time of massive failure and disappointment for farm people. In this chapter we shall attempt to sort out these conflicting aspects of the story, applying some elementary economic theory to understand the relation between agricultural development and the economic growth and transformation of the whole nation. Only recently have historians of American agriculture begun to apply economic theory and to test their hypotheses statistically. As a result, many important questions remain to be answered by further research. Given this state of knowledge, our discussion here must necessarily be incomplete and unsatisfactory, but perhaps we can suggest some ways in which a new approach to the subject might prove useful in future studies.

The output of agricultural products expanded rapidly in the post-Civil War era. Between 1869 and 1914, estimated wheat output increased from 290 to 897 million bushels, corn from 782 to 2524 million bushels, and oats from 284 to 1066 million bushels. The output of cotton, the great Southern cash crop and the nation's major export product, rose from 2.5 to 16.1 million bales of 500 pounds gross weight. The estimated slaughter of cattle went from 4.6 to 11.5 billion pounds of live weight, while the same measure for hogs increased only from 9.0 to 12.0, a reflection of a shift in consumer demand away from pork and toward beef as incomes increased. Various indexes of total farm output show an increase of about 200 percent during this period (Table 4.1), while the nation's population increased about 150 percent.

One source of this outpouring of farm products was an expansion of measurable inputs. Between 1870 and 1910, improved land in farms increased from 189 to 479 million acres. Investors also augmented the stocks

TABLE 4.1

GROSS AND NET FARM OUTPUT (MILLIONS OF 1929 DOLLARS)

Year	Gross Farm Output	Intermediate Products Consumed	Net Farm Output
1869	3,950	440	3510
1879	6,180	730	5450
1889	7,820	1000	6820
1899	9,920	1360	8560
1909	10,770	1620	9150

SOURCE. John W. Kendrick, *Productivity Trends in the United States* (Princeton, N. J.: Princeton University, 1961), p. 347.

TABLE 4.2
MATERIAL CAPITAL STOCKS IN AGRICULTURE
(MILLIONS OF 1929 DOLLARS)

Year	Total	Land	Structures	Machinery and Equipment	Work Stock	Inventories: Livestock	Inventories: Crops
1869	23,145	13,836	4,578	564	623	2697	847
1879	32,941	19,643	6,367	828	906	3643	1554
1889	40,132	23,863	7,006	1217	1274	4698	2074
1899	48,004	29,107	8,057	1900	1504	4770	2666
1909	55,295	31,735	11,255	3012	1739	4960	2594

SOURCE. John W. Kendrick, *Productivity Trends in the United States* (Princeton, N. J.: Princeton University, 1961), p. 367.

of other forms of material capital, increasing the stock of farm machinery and equipment fastest of all (Table 4.2). Though it became a progressively smaller part of the economy's total labor force, the farm labor force grew substantially in absolute terms, from 6.8 to 11.8 million workers.

As the ratio of capital of all kinds (material, human, and intellectual) to labor increased, output per man-hour rose. Between 1869 and 1914, net farm output per man-hour increased by about 50 percent. Using the same method employed in the Appendix, we can calculate that only about 30 percent of this increase was directly due to the accumulation of material capital, the remainder being attributable to (unmeasurable) human and intellectual capital accumulation. Inventions of improved reapers, threshers, plows, cultivators, and a great variety of other agricultural machinery and the progressive dissemination of these instruments apparently played major roles in augmenting agricultural technology, though "unembodied" technological advances such as the development of dry farming methods and better crop rotations were also evident, especially after 1900.

Regional differences in agricultural development were marked. In the South, 15 years or more were required merely to restore the losses sustained during the Civil War. Eugene Lerner has given an excellent summary:

> During the decade 1870–1880, the physical capital destroyed by war was replaced and by 1880, 15 years after the end of the war, most of the series reached or exceeded their 1860 levels. The number of cattle (other than cows) and acres of farms in the South were almost as great in 1880 as they were in 1860; the number of horses, mules, cows, and improved

> acres in the South ranged from 4 to 27 per cent higher. However, in spite of this growth of resources, the value series, though generally higher in 1880 than in 1870, were still below their 1860 levels. In 1880 the value of farms was 33 percent below its 1860 level, the value of farm implements was 31 percent lower and the value of livestock was down 24 per cent. . . . After the war, the South's farm labor force, predominantly Negro, became seriously disorganized, thus retarding the recovery of agriculture. . . . In addition to a disorganized labor force, the destruction of capital itself was a powerful force retarding agricultural expansion. Livestock could only be replaced with the passing of time, and even had the labor force been efficient, fields could not give abundant yields with a shortage of mules, plows, and horses. Moreover, capital markets must have been highly imperfect right after the war. Planters and farmers probably could not borrow to replace their depleted stock, and the principal source of funds available to farmers undoubtedly came from internal sources. Since output was low, savings were low, and recovery retarded. The curse of the poor is their poverty![1]

In the highly industrialized Northeastern states, agricultural output remained on a plateau, although its composition changed substantially as farmers shifted out of cereals and livestock into vegetables, fruits, dairy products, and poultry—outputs for which the rate of return depended crucially on immediate access to large urban markets. Elsewhere east of the Mississippi River, including the South, farm outputs expanded substantially, but the most rapid growth occurred west of the Mississippi, where settlement brought a vast and fertile area quickly under the plow. In 1869 the states west of approximately the 95th meridian produced about 6 percent of the nation's farm output; 40 years later they accounted for about 30 percent.

Before World War I, patterns of regional specialization clearly emerged. Cotton production, which continued to predominate in the "old" South, pushed westward into Texas and Oklahoma, the former state becoming the nation's leading producer. Winter wheat production concentrated in central Kansas and Nebraska, spring wheat in Minnesota and the Dakotas, while the "corn and hog belt" stretched from Ohio into eastern Nebraska. Cattle raising most heavily occupied an area between southern Texas and Chicago, the nation's greatest market for live beef cattle. Figures 4.1–4.5 give a good indication of the enduring patterns of regional specialization in agriculture, except that the distribution of wheat production changed substantially during 1900–1915 as California's output declined and that of Kansas and Nebraska increased.

1 Eugene M. Lerner, "Southern Output and Agricultural Income, 1860–1880," *Agricultural History*, XXXIII (July 1959), 117, 120, 121.

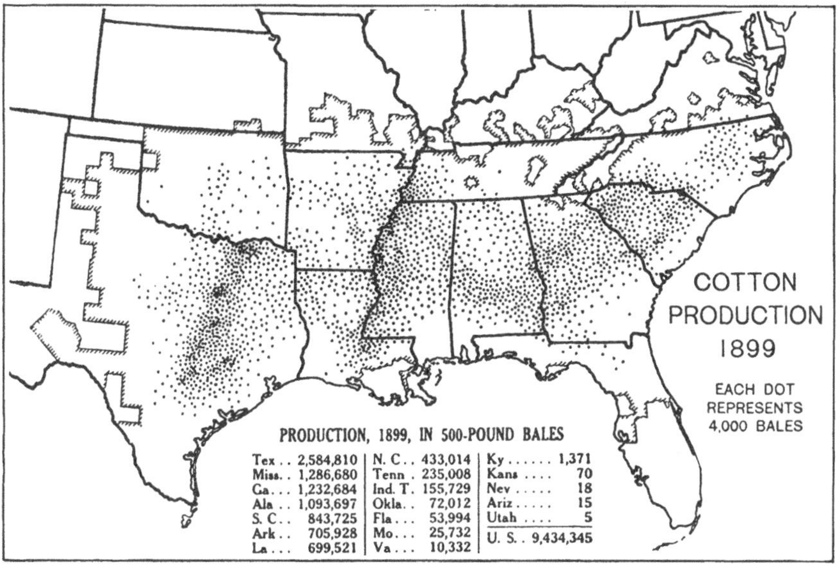

Figure 4.1 Spatial distribution of cotton production, 1899. *Source:* U. S. Department of Agriculture, *Yearbook, 1921* (Washington: Government Printing Office, 1922), p. 332.

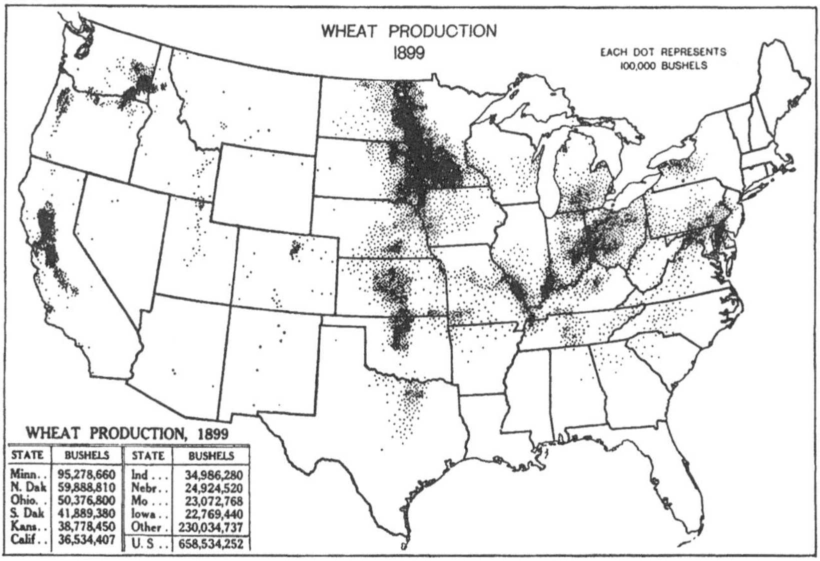

Figure 4.2 Spatial distribution of wheat production, 1899. *Source:* U. S. Department of Agriculture, *Yearbook, 1921* (Washington: Government Printing Office, 1922), p. 94.

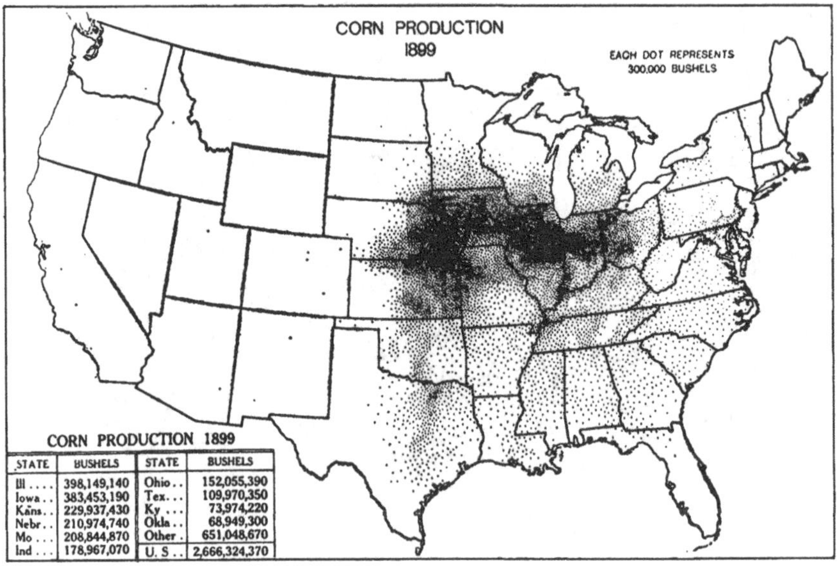

Figure 4.3 Spatial distribution of corn production, 1899. *Source:* U. S. Department of Agriculture, *Yearbook, 1921* (Washington: Government Printing Office, 1922), p. 173.

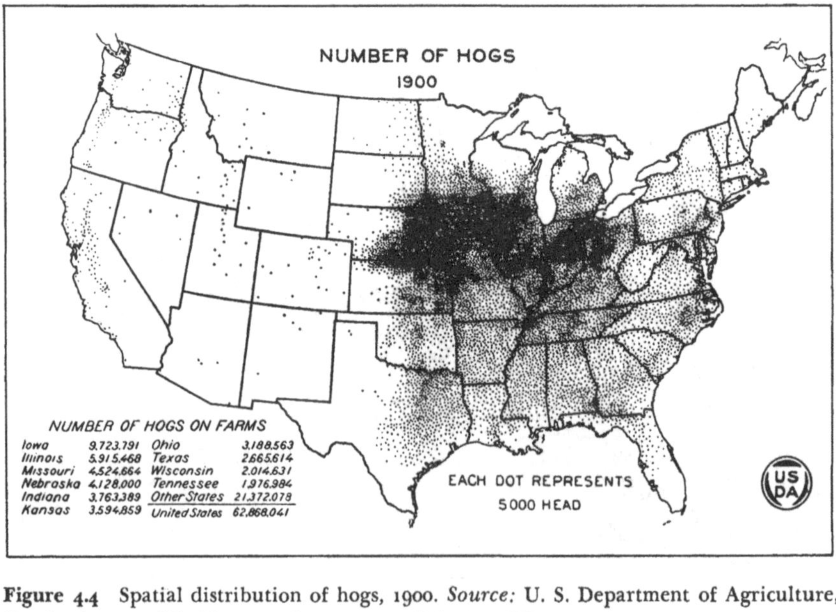

Figure 4.4 Spatial distribution of hogs, 1900. *Source:* U. S. Department of Agriculture, *Yearbook, 1922* (Washington: Government Printing Office, 1923), p. 190.

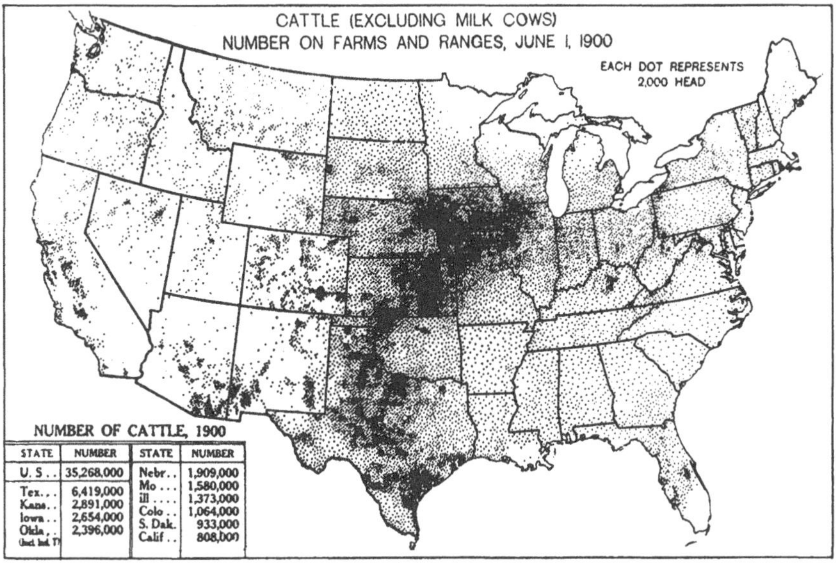

Figure 4.5 Spatial distribution of cattle, 1900. *Source:* U. S. Department of Agriculture, *Yearbook, 1921* (Washington: Government Printing Office, 1922), p. 237.

The productivity of farmers varied enormously from region to region, and the relative dispersion actually became greater between 1870 and 1910. In 1870 output per farmer was lowest in the South, highest in the Northeastern and Pacific Coast states; 40 years later the Southern states remained at the bottom, the Northeastern and Pacific states had fallen somewhat closer to the national average (although they remained substantially above it), and farmers in the Corn Belt, Great Plains, and Rocky Mountain regions had made major productivity gains.[2] Economic theory asserts that differences in output per worker result from differences in capital per worker. A major problem in testing this hypothesis is that stocks of human and intellectual capital cannot, in the present state of our knowledge, be measured. However, on the reasonable assumption that the accumulation of these kinds of capital is highly correlated with the accumulation of material capital, the hypothesis becomes as follows: output per worker and material capital, including land, per worker are directly related. Evidence shown in Figure 4.6 is remarkably consistent with this hypothesis, indicating that regional differences in the produc-

[2] Alvin S. Tostlebe, *Capital in Agriculture: Its Formation and Financing since 1870* (Princeton, N. J.: Princeton University, 1957), p. 95.

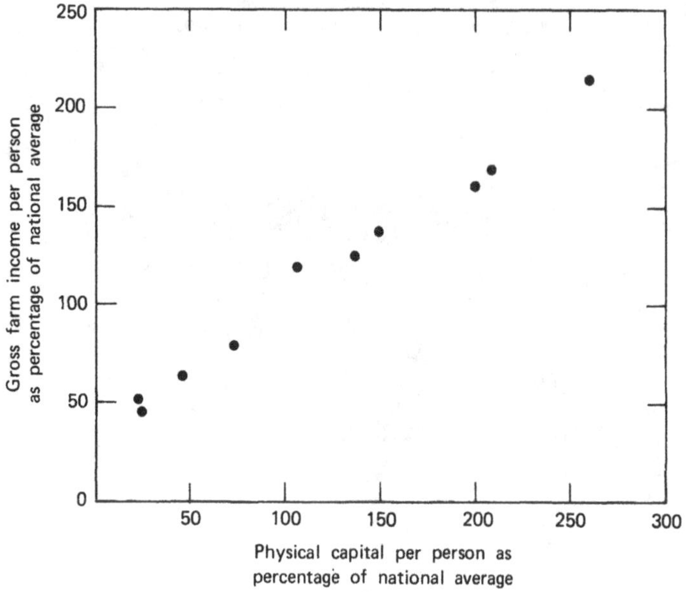

Figure 4.6 Gross farm income and physical capital per person engaged in agriculture, ten farming regions, 1910. *Source:* Alvin S. Tostlebe, *Capital in Agriculture: Its Formation and Financing Since 1870* (Princeton, N. J.: Princeton University, 1957), p. 95.

tivity of farmers can indeed be ascribed to differences in the amounts of capital each farmer had to assist him in production.

THE FARMER'S COMPLAINTS

From the late 1860's to the late 1890's numerous agrarian protest movements enlivened the American political scene. They included the Patrons of Husbandry, better known as the Grangers, whose political strength was concentrated in the Midwest in the 1870's; the Farmers' Alliances of the South and the Midwest in the 1880's; and the People's Party, or Populists, well represented in the South, the Great Plains, and the Far West in the 1890's. These movements differed in a variety of ways, but they had at least one significant belief in common: that the American farmer received less than his "fair share" of the national product. The explanations advanced to account for this alleged inequity were many: railroads charged the farmer rates that were "too high"; "speculators" and "land monopolists" engrossed the best of the public lands, while the homestead system that might have relieved the farmer played only a minor role in the disposition of the public domain; pernicious land-tenure systems, especially in the South, shackled the farmers and resulted in rapacious "mining" of the soil and destruction of its fertility; money lenders charged interest rates that were "too high"; a falling price level increased the real burden of debt repayment on the farmers' mortgages; farmers sold in competitive markets but purchased from "monopolists," and the result was a steady deterioration in their terms of trade; we might extend the list almost indefinitely.

To what extent were these charges valid? Unfortunately we cannot offer a complete answer, even though several generations of historians have concerned themselves with these issues. The early historians usually accepted the farmers' charges quite uncritically, and these biased interpretations color the accounts of widely used textbooks even today. Modern agricultural historians approach these subjects much more critically than did their predecessors, but the marshalling of evidence and its systematic analysis are still at an early stage. Although the evidence is sufficient for an evaluation of some of the farmers' complaints, it is almost nonexistent on others, and in some cases the most interesting questions have never been asked. We shall examine in turn each of the complaints catalogued above.

Railroad Rates

For 30 years after the Civil War, "excessive" railroad freight rates were a persistent grievance among farmers. During the past two decades, however, economic historians have generally dismissed this complaint as inconsistent with the facts. The historians are apparently unanimous in believing that railroad freight rates fell steeply and steadily throughout the Gilded Age. A recent study has shown, however, that the historians' belief, insofar as it concerns farmers, is probably false.[3] The evidence on which it rests is certainly inadequate, consisting almost exclusively of nominal rates. While these were typically falling, so were most other prices until the late 1890's, when the downward trend of the overall price level finally gave way to an upward trend. Since only the *relative* price of transportation is meaningful, nominal transport rates must be compared with a relevant price index. Making this comparison, we shall discover periods of increase as well as periods of decline in *real* freight

3 Robert Higgs, "Railroad Rates and the Populist Uprising," *Agricultural History*, XLIV (July 1970).

rates. In this case historians failed to ask the right question. They asked whether railroad rates had fallen, but that question is really meaningless. They should have asked whether railroad rates fell faster or slower than the prices farmers received for their products.

Figure 4.7 shows the movement over time of the wheat prices, corn prices, and cotton prices received by farmers divided by an index of railroad freight rates for the 1867–1915 period. Given the descriptions of

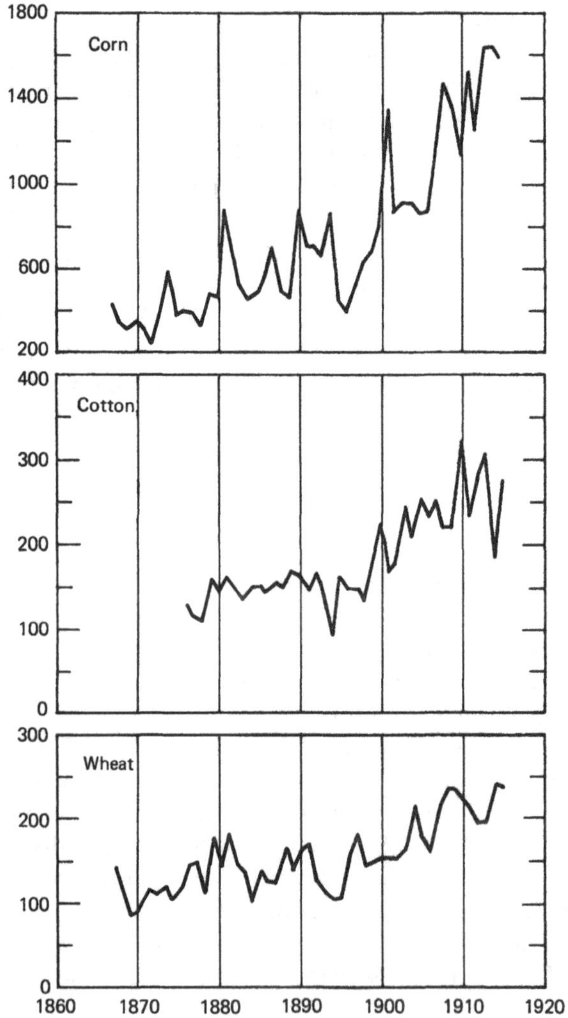

Figure 4.7 Indexes of farm price/railroad rate ratios. *Source:* Robert Higgs, "Railroad Rates and the Populist Uprising," *Agricultural History,* XLIV (July 1970), 295.

recent historians, we would expect that, despite year-to-year fluctuations, the trends of the curves would move steadily upward. It is evident that they do not. In fact, three aspects of the series stand out: first, they vary enormously from year to year; second, before 1897 the trend is approximately horizontal;[4] and third, real improvement in the farmers' position begins only in the late 1890's. The depression of the mid-1890's put growers of all three crops at a particular disadvantage. Wheat growers in 1894 were in their worst position in the entire period, with the exception of the years 1869, 1870, and 1874. Corn growers in 1896 had not faced such unfavorable terms of trade with the railroads since 1878. For cotton, where reliable data are unavailable before 1876, the low mark for the entire period occurred in 1894. It must be emphasized, however, that more is involved here than farmers suffering from the depression of the 1890's. Even if we consider only the years before 1893, the data still fail to show any substantial (statistically significant) improvement in the farmers' position. In brief, farmers did not benefit from lower transportation charges over the three decades before 1897. The amounts of cotton, corn, or wheat exchanged for a ton-mile of railroad transportation remained substantially unchanged throughout the Gilded Age. This finding makes the farmers' complaint about "high" railroad freight rates somewhat more comprehensible.

Transport charges were an important part of farmers' costs. In some areas of the Great Plains and the Far West the freight charges incurred in moving crops to a market might absorb as much as half of the crops' value at that market. Under such circumstances the failure of transport rates to decline by more than 10 to 15 percent while farm prices were collapsing by 30 to 50 percent was a genuine economic source of farm distress in the mid-1890's. Where transport charges were a relatively high proportion of farm costs—for example, in Kansas, Nebraska, and the Dakotas—the Populists were most active and successful, while relatively little protest came from areas where transport charges were less important, such as Iowa, Missouri, and Illinois. And most importantly, the experience of the previous 25 years gave farmers no reason to expect an imminent improvement. It is difficult to say whether they objected that rates were higher than they "should" have been or whether they considered their position to have been worsening, but one thing is clear: they recognized no recent improvement with respect to railroad rates. Notably, the two decades preceding the World War, for which the data show such substantial improvement in the farmers' position (Figure 4.7), also witnessed the

[4] In a statistical sense, the hypothesis that the pre-1897 trend is horizontal cannot be rejected at customary levels of confidence. For the statistical test, see *ibid.*, pp. 294, 296, n. 17.

disappearance of widespread agrarian unrest. Of course, we should not attribute the decline of agrarian radicalism exclusively to declining real railroad rates, since other aspects of the rural economy also improved during the two decades preceding the American entry into World War I; but neither was this correspondence entirely accidental.

"Land Monopolists," "Speculators," and the Homestead System

In 1862 Congress passed the Homestead Act, which provided that 160 acres of the public domain might be acquired by a settler if he lived on the land or cultivated it for five consecutive years. The federal government continued, however, to sell some land at auction as well as to donate land to the states and to railroad companies as subsidies. Because several different methods of transferring the public domain to private owners were simultaneously employed, the disposition of federal lands in the post-Civil War era has been characterized as occurring within an "incongruous land system." In a famous article, the historian Paul Gates criticized this system, asserting that competing methods of disposition subverted the true purpose of the Homestead Act and that "speculation and land monopolization continued after its adoption as widely perhaps as before."[5] This interpretation, which continues to influence historians, suffers from a fundamental misconception of how a market economy operates.

Economists use the term "monopoly" to describe a market within which only one seller offers a well-defined product. Certainly, when historians speak of "land monopoly" they do not mean that all the land belonged to a single owner. Economists also use the expression "monopoly power" to denote an attribute of a seller who provides such a large part of the market supply that by varying the amount he offers for sale he can affect the market price of the product. Certainly no one in the nineteenth century ever owned enough land to be able to affect the price of land in general. Millions of different owners held land, and even the very largest —like William Chapman, who held over a million acres of California land in the 1870's, or the land-grant railroad companies, which held much more—were incapable of influencing the average price of land; their holdings were simply insignificant in comparison with the total stock of land. Of course, an owner might set any price he liked for his own land, but that is trivial, because if he set the price too high no one would buy. The market for land was everywhere highly competitive. What the his-

[5] Paul Wallace Gates, "The Homestead Law in an Incongruous Land System," *American Historical Review*, XLI (July 1936), 655.

torian really means when he speaks of a "land monopolist" is an owner of an unusually large acreage, sometimes no more than 500 or 1000 acres. That the size of holdings varied widely is common knowledge, however, and the expression "land monopolist" neither adds anything to that knowledge nor is useful in analysis. The term is simply pejorative and ought to be abandoned.

Historians have similarly erred by using the term "speculator" to characterize a person who buys solely with the intent to resell and not to cultivate. The objection to this usage is that *in a private property system every owner of an asset is necessarily a speculator* in the sense that he bears the risk of reductions in the value of the asset but hopes that the value will rise. Of course land speculators purchased the public domain; every purchaser was a speculator. Allan Bogue has observed that "certainly the man who came west, bought a tract of the size that he thought necessary for his farming operations, and then tilled it for the rest of his life was rare indeed. The more common picture was one of several moves or repeated purchases and sales."[6] And the settler who continued to hold his land was no less a speculator than his neighbor who sold out and moved on, but merely one who perceived that the highest rate of return could be obtained by continuing to hold what he had. Some purchased large acreages, others small acreages; all speculated. To describe the large purchasers as speculators and the small purchasers as "actual settlers" obscures the identity of their reasons for holding land: to obtain the highest possible rate of return. Bogue also found in his excellent study of agriculture in Illinois and Iowa that "from the very beginning, large numbers of settlers and farmers in this region had a strong commercial orientation. They sought to maximize the returns from their farming operations, and, if in the early years cash itself was scarce, they undoubtedly evaluated the material possessions that they accumulated—their lands and livestock—in terms of money."[7] Rational people, it might be added, could hardly have calculated their real incomes in any other way.

The great bulk of the land put into cultivation after 1865 was purchased from federal and state governments and from land-grant railroads; less than one fifth was homesteaded. This fact has led some historians to conclude that the Homestead Act was a failure. Perhaps a more interesting question concerns the effect of the homestead system on the economic growth of the nation. We might ask: was the national product greater or

6 Allan G. Bogue, *From Prairie to Corn Belt* (Chicago: University of Chicago, 1963), p. 51.

7 *Ibid.*, p. 193.

less as a result of the homestead system? Economic theory provides a straightforward answer.

For considering this question, it is most useful to conceive of the homestead system as one of many possible ways of transferring ownership of the land from the federal government to private individuals. Any system of transferring ownership—whether homesteading, outright sales, or something else—required the commitment of resources: land must be surveyed, titles established, and records kept in any event. The opportunity cost of the resources involved in such activities constituted the "transaction cost" of transferring property rights. But the homestead system of transferring ownership involved additional transaction costs, for it required the recipient of the land to live on or cultivate the land for five consecutive years before he could receive the title; moreover, the law provided that a maximum of 160 acres could be acquired. In effect, these provisions of the Homestead Act, to the extent that they were enforced, required the recipient to combine certain minimum amounts of labor and capital with the land. It is certainly conceivable that in many instances the required commitments of labor and capital exceeded the economically optimal amounts. For example, in areas suited only for grazing, the homestead system dictated too much labor and capital relative to land. Under such circumstances the opportunity cost of the economically excessive resources constituted a pure transaction cost of transferring ownership to the private individual.

Some scholars have argued that the homestead system had the effect of luring too much labor and capital into agriculture, that the system misallocated resources and thereby reduced the national product. This argument is correct only in the transaction-cost sense noted above; and such misallocation must surely have been negligible in its effect on the national product. The important point is that whatever resource misallocation did occur was transitory. Had the land been sold at auction instead of being homesteaded, it would have commanded a certain price based on its ability to contribute toward earning the farmer an income. That price is exactly what the land commanded once the private owner had acquired the title through homesteading. Therefore, whether the land was sold or homesteaded, its price was ultimately the same, and hence farmers combined labor and capital with it in exactly the same proportions in both cases. Homesteading induced no long-term misallocation of resources.

The real importance of the homestead system was that it transferred wealth to the recipients of the land and away from federal taxpayers, whose taxes could have been less had the land been sold. Whether this redistribution of wealth affected patterns of saving and investment in a way that altered the growth path of the economy is unknown. In fact, scholars are at present uncertain whether this wealth transfer made the distribution of total wealth more or less equal, for little is known about the wealth of those who acquired the homesteads, and widespread fraud within the homestead system complicates research on the subject.

Ownership, Tenure, and Efficiency

No one considers it paradoxical that today many wealthy people rent rather than own their houses or apartments. For various reasons some people simply prefer to rent; and the decision to rent or purchase is really a decision about the form in which people wish to hold their wealth. Many historians, however, continue to use the extent of farm tenancy as an index of farm distress, relying upon statistics like those in Table 4.3 to illustrate their argument. Such statistics are valuable, but for a different reason; they are certainly not a reliable index of farm distress.

Why did many farmers rent rather than buy? The answers are many, but probably one is most important: they lacked the money to buy and were unable to borrow on acceptable terms. One should not, however,

TABLE 4.3

PERCENTAGE DISTRIBUTION OF FARMS BY CLASS OF TENURE, 1890

Region	Cultivated by Owners	Rented for Fixed Money Value	Rented for Shares of Products
North Atlantic	82	8	10
South Atlantic	62	13	26
North Central	77	8	16
South Central	62	14	24
Western	88	5	7
United States	72	10	18

SOURCE. *United States Census, 1890: Agriculture* (Washington: Government Printing Office, 1895), pp. 118–19. Percentages may not sum to 100 because of rounding. Regions are defined as follows. *North Atlantic*: Maine, New Hampshire, Vermont, Massachusetts, Rhode Island, Connecticut, New York, New Jersey, and Pennsylvania. *South Atlantic*: Delaware, Maryland, District of Columbia, Virginia, West Virginia, North Carolina, South Carolina, Georgia, and Florida. *North Central*: Ohio, Indiana, Illinois, Michigan, Wisconsin, Minnesota, Iowa, Missouri, North Dakota, South Dakota, Nebraska, and Kansas. *South Central*: Kentucky, Tennessee, Alabama, Mississippi, Louisiana, Texas, Oklahoma, and Arkansas. *Western*: all other states and territories within the continental United States.

jump to the conclusion that such men were dispossessed former owners or necessarily poor. Farms were expensive, varying from less than a dollar to more than a hundred dollars per acre depending on the time and place. At these prices a hundred-acre farm ranged from $100 to $10,000, substantial amounts at a time when farm laborers typically earned less than a dollar a day. Many tenants were young men accumulating the savings that would ultimately permit them to purchase a farm. Newcomers to an area, even though they had the money to buy immediately, often rented for a year or two while searching for information about the relative merits of lands for sale. In the South tenancy provided a way to bring the labor of millions of penniless former slaves together with the lands and tools of the former slave owners. It should be noted, however, that in all the regions, including the South, at least 62 percent of the farms in 1890 were cultivated by their owners (Table 4.3).

Within the two great classes of tenancy, cash rental and sharecropping, a large variety of distinct subtypes of rental arrangement existed. What determined the form of these contracts? Steven Cheung has proposed the following hypothesis:

> [T]he choice of contracts is determined by weighing the gains from risk dispersions and the costs of contracting associated with different contracts. Two factors appear to be important in explaining different patterns of contractual choices in different localities. First, different physical attributes of crops and types of climate often result in different variances of outputs in different agricultural areas. Second, different legal arrangements . . . affect the variances of incomes as well as affecting transaction costs for the contracting parties.[8]

To clarify this hypothesis, consider two areas identical except that one is subject to a larger variation in rainfall from year to year. Because erratic rainfall increases the risk of occasional crop failure, we would expect sharecropping to be a more prevalent form of lease in the area of erratic rainfall than in the other area. Share leases allow the tenant to shift some of the risk onto the landlord, while cash leases give the landlord a fixed money rent whether crops be good or bad and hence place all the risk on the tenant. Tenants therefore demand share leases and persuade landlords to shoulder some of the risk by offering them higher shares.

Contracts must be enforced as well as made, and the costs of enforcement vary with the form of the contract. Bogue found that in Illinois and Iowa,

[8] Steven N. S. Cheung, "Transaction Costs, Risk Aversion, and the Choice of Contractual Arrangements," *Journal of Law and Economics*, XII (April 1969), 29–30.

> share leases probably were always more common than cash leases. Under such agreements the landlord shared the uncertainties of nature. Absentee landlords, however, always preferred a cash payment, since share agreements were difficult to supervise from a distance. Declining grain prices during the last quarter of the nineteenth century and an active demand for rental farms also inclined the landlords to ask for cash rather than share agreements.[9]

Local landlords were more likely to accept a share lease because their proximity to the land allowed them more cheaply to ensure that the tenant did not dispose of some of the crop before the shares were divided.

It seems clear that contract forms and terms varied with changes in the relative supply of and demand for contracts of a particular sort. This hypothesis furnishes a basis for improving our understanding of land tenure patterns and should be tested more extensively by future research.

For at least a century, students of land tenure systems have asserted that sharecropping is inimical to improvement of the soil because the tenant has no secure claim to the long-term returns from his investments in the land, and, especially in the South, they have blamed the deterioration of soil quality on the prevalence of sharecropping. Data shown in Table 4.3 cast doubt on this interpretation. Most of the farmers everywhere, including the South, owned their farms, and the returns from an investment would have accrued directly to them. Why did landowners not invest more in preserving the fertility of their land? One interpretation is that until the late nineteenth century farmers of all classes, both owners and tenants, paid little attention to preserving the fertility of their land. And such action, or lack of action, was probably quite rational, at least from a private wealth-maximizing point of view. When virgin land was cheaply available farther west, it simply did not pay to invest in fertilization and other costly improvements; a more lucrative strategy was to "mine" the soil and then move on. Notably, the farmers of Georgia and the Carolinas, far from the frontier and faced with relatively high costs of migration westward to virgin soil, were the first to make major applications of commercial fertilizers.[10]

The economic theory of share tenancy provides an additional argument against the view that sharecropping was especially damaging to the soil. In Cheung's words:

9 Bogue, 1963, *op. cit.*, p. 60.

10 Fred A. Shannon, *The Farmer's Last Frontier: Agriculture, 1860–1897* (New York: Holt, Rinehart, and Winston, 1945), pp. 115, 169–72. A recent study found that during 1880–1960 "variations in the fertilizer-land price ratio alone explain almost 90 percent of the variation in fertilizers." See Yujiro Hayami and V. W. Ruttan, "Factor Prices and Technical Change in Agricultural Development: The United States and Japan, 1880–1960," *Journal of Political Economy*, LXXVIII (Sept./Oct. 1970), 1133.

> It does not matter whether the landlord stipulates that the tenant is to invest more in land and charges a lower rental percentage or whether the landowner invests in land himself and charges the tenant a higher rental percentage; the investment will be made if it leads to a higher rental annuity.[11]

And again Bogue's evidence for the prairie region is consistent with the hypothesis: "The less improved a farm was, the greater the chance that the tenant could negotiate leasing terms that would reward him for improvements."[12]

These bits of hypothesis and evidence suggest very strongly that the whole subject of land tenure in United States history needs to be restudied in the light of recent advances in economic theory. Until that is done, our understanding of the relative efficiency of different tenure arrangements must remain highly imperfect. It now appears that in this field, as in so many others, failure to consider the influence of competition within the constraints of private property rights has led to errors of analysis.

Interest Rates, Debts, and Deflation

During the last third of the nineteenth century, agrarian radicals increasingly vilified the moneylender: the agent of an Eastern, or even international, "conspiracy," this "hyena-faced Shylock" tricked innocent farmers into borrowing funds they did not "need" at interest rates that were "too high," his object being to "rob" them of their lands through foreclosures. This description is an obvious caricature, but the business of mortgage lending was a source of concern also to less impassioned observers. Fortunately, recent research on this subject sheds considerable light on the problems surrounding farm mortgages.

Why did farmers mortgage their lands? The answers are legion, for farmers used the funds obtained on the security of farm real estate to pay alimony, erect tombstones, provide daughters with dowry, and enter horses in races—to mention only a small fraction of the more interesting uses. The bulk of the funds borrowed, however, was put to more prosaic, and more productive, uses. In areas of recent settlement farmers frequently borrowed to purchase livestock, machinery, and other farm equipment, but the principal use of funds everywhere was apparently the acquisition of real estate. In short, farmers borrowed on the security of their present

[11] Steven N. S. Cheung, "Private Property Rights and Sharecropping," *Journal of Political Economy*, LXXVI (Nov./Dec. 1968), 1121.

[12] Bogue, 1963, *op. cit.*, p. 61.

land holdings in order to acquire even more land. Such borrowing was concentrated in periods of prosperity and hardly qualifies as an index of agricultural distress.

Though moneylenders were often accused of being "monopolists," competition was active in most areas of the country during the 1870's and grew even more intense over time. In Illinois and Iowa, Bogue found that

> by 1870 at least, most country towns had several agents competing for the mortgage business. The farmer with good security and a fine personal reputation in the community might play them off against each other and win concessions on the interest rate, the amount of commission charged by the agent, or in the form and type of paper. . . . [I]f the lenders of one town combined they might find themselves undercut by the energetic agents of some nearby prairie center, as well as by petty lenders.[13]

The accumulation of savings in the Eastern states, in combination with a relatively high demand for credit in the Western agricultural areas, gave rise to a new kind of business agent, the Western mortgage broker. Hundreds of these brokers organized during the 1870's and 1880's. Many failed during the depression of the 1890's, but some survived to facilitate the continuing transfer of funds from an area of low interest rates to one of relatively high interest rates. The broker's task was essentially the collection and sale of information. He sought out potential credit-worthy borrowers and willing lenders and brought them together in mutually agreeable loan contracts; that is, he informed them of one another's demands. The result was that Easterners earned higher rates of return on their savings, Westerners paid lower rates of interest on their loans, and the mortgage broker's commission gave him an income for his trouble. More generally, the broker's information-gathering and -disseminating services allowed a more efficient functioning of the credit market on a national scale.

The interest rate on farm mortgages tended to fall everywhere throughout the last quarter of the nineteenth century, though rate differences among places persisted, reflecting differences in the risks attending loans. In the areas of Illinois, Iowa, Kansas, and Nebraska for which Bogue obtained evidence, the interest rate on farm mortgages fell by at least one half during the last third of the nineteenth century, and the same downward trend was probably the case elsewhere. In Texas, "competition among the lending agencies was keen by 1886 at least. . . . By 1888 there was talk of combination to halt the decline in lending rates, but there was evidently no concerted action on this score."[14] As many

13 *Ibid.*, p. 174.

14 Allan G. Bogue, *Money at Interest* (Ithaca, N. Y.: Cornell University, 1955), p. 160.

states passed usury laws placing an unreasonably low ceiling on the rate of interest, lenders devised a variety of commission charges to circumvent the restriction, and only detailed studies can reveal what the full interest rate paid by the farmer actually was. J. B. Watkins, a mortgage broker who loaned millions of dollars in the Great Plains area, obtained interest of 16 to 17 percent in the mid-1870's. Bogue found that "in all probability the total rate stood between 10 and 12 percent in western Kansas during the late 1880's. Meanwhile rates had dropped in central Kansas, where money could be obtained on the security of good land at a total cost of between 8 and 9 percent."[15] By the turn of the century rates were in the neighborhood of 5 to 6 percent over large areas of the Midwest. Stories of mortgage interest rates reaching 40 or 50 percent, of which the Populist orators were so fond, were certainly atypical, if true at all.

Interest rates fell for two reasons. First, with increasing accumulation of savings, and new business agents like the Western mortgage brokers and the representatives of insurance companies to channel these funds where they would earn the highest rate of return, competition among lenders forced interest rates down. Farm mortgages were generally drawn for terms of one to five years, and when extensions or new loans were negotiated farmers usually contracted at a new, lower rate of interest. A second reason for the decline in rates was the general downward trend in prices during the three decades before 1897. General deflation made a dollar increasingly more valuable in terms of its purchasing power over goods. The *real rate of interest* was the nominal rate adjusted for changes in the purchasing power of money.[16] For example, the farmer who borrowed at 10 percent for a year during which the price level declined by 5 percent paid the same *real* rate as the farmer who borrowed at 15.8 percent for a year during which prices were stable. Recognizing that deflation seemed to be a fact of life, many farmers no doubt bargained with lenders for a lower rate of interest in anticipation of falling prices.

Falling prices inspired much complaint among agrarian radicals. In a recent study, Robert Fogel and Jack Rutner have argued, however, that the increased real burden of debt repayment attributable to falling prices was almost negligible for farmers in general. "[C]apital losses on mortgages due to unanticipated changes in the price level had only a slight effect on the average profit of farmers. [See Table 4.4.] . . .

15 *Ibid.*, p. 272.

16 "The relationship between the 'real' interest rate, r, in money units for a stable price level, and the actual market interest rate, R, in money units, if the price level is *known* to be changing at the rate of p percent a year, is: $R = (1 + r)(1 + p) - 1$." See Armen A. Alchian and William R. Allen, *University Economics*, 2d ed. (Belmont, Calif.: Wadsworth, 1967), pp. 437-38.

TABLE 4.4

AVERAGE ANNUAL PERCENTAGE CAPITAL GAIN ON FARMS

Period	Without Adjustment	Adjusted for Loss on Mortgages
1869–79	2.8	2.3
1879–89	2.8	2.6
1889–99	−0.4	−0.4

SOURCE. Robert William Fogel and Jack Rutner, "The Efficiency Effects of Federal Land Policy, 1850–1900: A Report of Some Provisional Findings," University of Chicago Center for Mathematical Studies in Business and Economics, Report 7027, June 1970, p. 17. The adjustment is made on the assumption that price changes were never anticipated; the adjustment is therefore an upper limit.

[T]he debt to asset ratio was low (about 13 percent) for most farmers. It was only the farmer with a high debt to asset ratio who was badly hurt by the declining price level. But such farmers were atypical."[17] We need not dispute this finding to maintain that the combination of deflation and heavy indebtedness probably hurt the farmers of some areas badly; and after all, farmers who joined actively in the various agrarian protest movements were also atypical. Heavy indebtedness was typical of newly settled areas. Walter Nugent's careful study of Kansas revealed that "mortgage distress was not only real, but particularly severe for the Populists."[18] And the same conditions probably prevailed in Nebraska, the Dakotas, and other Western strongholds of Populism, though the quantitative research that would test this hypothesis remains to be done.

Relative Prices and Incomes

Farmers often complained that the prices they paid declined more slowly or rose more rapidly than the prices they received. During some short periods their claim was surely valid, but they were seldom heard from when the reverse obtained, as was also the case from time to time. What we would like to know is the *trend* of prices paid relative to prices

17 Robert William Fogel and Jack Rutner, "The Efficiency Effects of Federal Land Policy, 1850–1900: A Report of Some Provisional Findings," University of Chicago Center for Mathematical Studies in Business and Economics, Report 7027, June 1970, p. 19.

18 Walter T. K. Nugent, "Some Parameters of Populism," *Agricultural History*, XL (Oct. 1966), 264.

received by farmers. Unfortunately such statistics were not collected before 1910, so proxies will have to serve. Several price series exist for goods at wholesale markets; they do not tell us exactly what we would like to know because they do not take into account the costs of getting farm products from the farmer to the wholesale market and of carrying nonfarm goods in the opposite direction. We know, however, that transport charges during the three decades before 1897 probably fell on average about as rapidly as the prices received by farmers for wheat, corn, and cotton; on the assumption that this decline applied equally to the carriage of both farm and nonfarm goods, it is probably safe to use the wholesale price ratios to indicate the trend of relative prices received and paid by farmers. Wholesale price series show the trend of farm prices falling about as fast as the trend of nonfarm prices before 1897; if any difference existed it was that nonfarm prices fell more rapidly than farm prices. In cases where the quality of nonfarm goods increased substantially, the farmer's true terms of trade improved even faster than the price ratios indicate. During the two decades before the American entry into World War I, farm prices clearly advanced more rapidly than nonfarm prices.

Merely knowing the trend of relative prices, however, tells us nothing about farmers' relative incomes. A farmer's income depended not only on the price he received for his output, but also on the amount of output he produced. During the post-Civil War era, farm productivity did not grow as fast as nonfarm productivity. Therefore, during the period 1865–96, when relative prices were approximately unchanged, the average farmer's income grew at a slower rate than that of the average nonfarm producer. Although farmers became substantially better off in absolute terms, they became worse off relative to others. And even though relative prices turned in the farmer's favor after 1896, relative farm incomes might still have declined, because farm output per man-hour hardly increased at all during the next two decades. The overall trends mask substantial differences among regions: farmers' incomes rose hardly at all in the Northeastern states, somewhat more rapidly in the South, and fastest in the Midwest.

Production for home use and receipts from sales were not the sum of the farmer's income. Farmers owned large stocks of capital, mainly land, the real value of which steadily appreciated. To find the farmer's total income in any year, we must add to the receipts from sales and the implicit value of production for home use an amount equal to the appreciation of the farm capital stock. The amount added in this way would certainly be substantial for some times and places, especially for areas in an early stage of settlement or for most areas in the early twentieth century, when land values appreciated rapidly. Farmers obviously took such capital gains into account in deciding on their best course of action. A failure to consider capital gains as part of income has marred much discussion of the relative income of the farmer; that such gains were typically "automatically reinvested" is beside the point. Even when we correctly compute the farmer's income, however, we find that it is still lower on the average than that of nonfarm income earners. The major consequence of this difference was that farm people seeking to better themselves migrated in a steadily swelling stream into nonfarm occupations.

A Summary and Some Additional Grievances

Our survey of the farmer's major complaints has yielded no striking conclusions. During the late nineteenth century particular groups of farmers, though not farmers in general, were hurt by a combination of falling prices and heavy indebtedness; the homestead system probably contributed to a slight, temporary misallocation of resources but had little or no effect on either the national income or the development of agriculture generally; interest rates fell markedly, while the relative price of railroad transport and the farmer's overall terms of trade were approximately stable. Taken together, all these findings do not amount to much, certainly not enough to enlarge substantially our understanding of nineteenth century agrarian radicalism. Farmers' incomes, however, did not increase as fast as did the incomes of nonfarm producers, a difference attributable to the relatively slow advance of farm productivity. Complaint, political protest, and migration were the predictable consequences of this widening gap, but any conclusions must be qualified by substantial differences among crops, times, and places.

Perhaps other sources of unrest were also at work. Farmers generally led quite isolated lives. Unlike the practice in Europe, where farmers lived together in villages and went out each day to tend their fields in the surrounding countryside, the American farmer generally lived on his farm, a half mile or more from the closest neighbor and several miles from the nearest town. The loneliness of such a life must have cut deeper as the number of urban alternatives grew and became more accessible. Farm women appear to have suffered most from the social barrenness of the countryside, but perhaps the historians have merely recorded disproportionately the women's expressions of grievance and both sexes suffered equally. One hundred and sixty acres was a small world, and many had less.

Probably greater sources of unrest were the extreme instability and consequent unpredictability of farm production. Insects, diseases, droughts, prairie fires, floods, hailstorms and blizzards—all took their erratic toll from year to year. Yields fluctuated madly. Because these random occurrences affected differently the various parts of the supplying area—which might be national or even international, depending on the crop—the farmer could not expect that a low yield would necessarily be offset by a high price. It might be, but then it might not be; one could only hope. Farmers generally understood the reasons for this instability but could neither control nor reduce it.

Economists now recognize that certainty itself is for most people an economic good. When faced with two alternative occupations, both having the same expected average earnings over the long run but one fluctuating wildly around the mean while the other remains stable from year to year, most people prefer the job with stable earnings. Expected average earnings are the same in each, but one offers greater certainty. Earnings in nonfarm occupations were by no means perfectly predictable in the post-Civil War era; urban workers knew the meaning of unemployment and wage cuts. But the uncertainty surrounding farm production was substantially greater than that associated with most types of nonfarm work. It is reasonable to conclude, therefore, that farmers migrated to nonfarm jobs seeking greater certainty as well as higher real incomes.

THE LEARNING PROCESS IN AGRICULTURE

The American farmer in the post-Civil War era necessarily had to make frequent decisions. What crops should he plant, when, and in what proportions? Should he buy or sell livestock? Should he purchase or hire a newly devised implement? Should he buy or rent more land? Should he use fertilizer, and if so, what kind and how much? Not even the farmers of the older states could avoid such choices, for the technological and economic environments within which they operated changed constantly. They had acquired familiarity with the topography and climate of their areas through long experience, but new competition from the West, the growth of nearby urban markets, new technology, and a host of other changes forced adjustment on them if they were to continue to earn their accustomed rate of return. In the newly settled areas the range of necessary choices was considerably wider. The weather, insects, crop and animal diseases, length of growing season, soil conditions—all these were different, and hence new choices were required. A Norwegian immigrant wrote from Iowa: "I can truthfully say that the only things that seem to be the same are the fleas, for their bite is as sharp and penetrating here as elsewhere."[19]

The rapid growth and transformation of the economy and the sweep of settlement across half a continent in less than 50 years created an environment of extreme flux for the farmer. He had to adjust to the new conditions. But how? Distinguishing the influence of long-run shifts in supply or demand from the temporary vagaries of the market was a difficult task. Quickly determining the best production methods or crops in a newly settled area called for greater scientific prowess than the scientists of the day—much less the farmers—could boast. Yet new choices were made that ultimately resulted in a more or less successful adjustment to the new economic and natural environments. A *learning process* lay at the heart of these adjustments. The economic theory of learning, which seeks to explain both the creation of new and the dissemination of old knowledge, has only recently been much explored, but already it promises some useful clues for the historian.

The creation of new knowledge can occur in several ways: within special research institutions, through individual experimentation, and by learning from experience. In the first two cases resources are deliberately committed to the search for new knowledge; in the third case the knowledge is a by-product of efforts made for other purposes. The quantity of resources committed to seeking new knowledge within research institutions or through individual experimentation depends on the expected rate of return, though in the former case political influences often intervene, because the institutions are publicly supported and administered. The output of new knowledge is, on the average, proportional to the input of resources. The output of new knowledge acquired as a by-product of production experience depends crucially on the kind of production. Some activities almost inevitably involve a good deal of learning, while others might be pursued indefinitely without yielding an intellectual by-product.

The United States Department of Agriculture, created in 1862, and the state experiment stations, established by the Hatch Act of 1887, were the principal research institutions concerned with agriculture during the post-Civil War era. Until the twentieth century, however, their output of new knowledge had little effect in expanding agricultural technology. The land-grant colleges, established by the Morrill Act of 1862, likewise had little effect. They trained a few students and provided speakers for farmers' meetings, but throughout most of the period they

[19] Bogue, 1963, p. 238.

occupied themselves with establishing the basic curriculum and staff that would allow them later to make a genuine contribution to education and research. Of course, these institutions, especially the Department of Agriculture and the colleges, had other duties besides research, and their success or failure should be evaluated in terms that include their other activities as well.

Lacking institutions to provide a substantial flow of new knowledge, American farmers were left to their own devices—individual experimentation and learning from experience. In a sense, farmers were always experimenting, for they seldom conducted their affairs in precisely the same way from one year to the next, but the instability of nature and of markets made the results of such inherent experimentation difficult to evaluate. Deliberate, controlled experimentation was almost exclusively the province of the wealthy farmer, and for good reason. Lacking a body of scientifically established principles as a starting point, the farmer who experimented assumed substantial risks. For the rich farmer with a large and perhaps geographically dispersed holding, a few failures did not lead to disaster, but the small farmer simply could not afford to take such chances. The problem was not, as too often asserted, that the bulk of the farmers were backward, stubborn, or too unenlightened to see the virtue of trying new methods. In general, the small farmer's traditional conservatism and skepticism about "book farming" were rational attitudes toward the assumption of large risks.

Learning from experience was open to all farmers, but the rate at which they acquired new knowledge depended crucially on the technical and economic characteristics of the crop. Nathan Rosenberg has suggested that the difference between the rates of learning in the Midwest and in the South might be explained in these terms:

> Some crops require an unskilled labour input performing nothing but simple, routinized, repetitive tasks—e.g., cotton. . . . [M]idwestern U.S. agriculture has provided a radically different experience. The pattern of agricultural activity in the American midwest was of such a nature that it developed a high degree of commercial and technical sophistication on the part of the labour inputs. Much of the explanation lies in the fact that this was an agriculture centered on livestock husbandry which required a highly efficient and sophisticated system of managerial decision-making. . . . The midwestern farm is often a fairly elaborate enterprise where the decision-maker must be close to the detailed day to day operations of the farm and which require a familiarity with market phenomena and a wide range of technical skills. Midwestern farming has therefore produced effective managers and people well-versed in mechanical skills. . . .[20]

[20] Nathan Rosenberg, "Neglected Dimensions in the Analysis of Economic Change,"

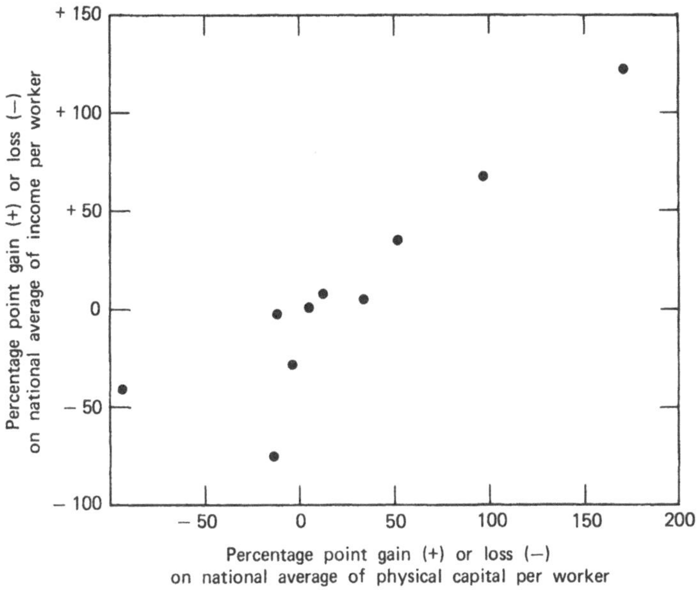

Figure 4.8 Relation between physical capital accumulation and growth of income in agriculture, ten farming regions, 1870–1910. *Source:* Alvin S. Tostlebe, *Capital in Agriculture: Its Formation and Financing since 1870* (Princeton, N. J.: Princeton University, 1957), p. 95.

It might be added that apparently the purely technical difficulties of mechanizing the harvest of the major Southern crops, cotton and corn, were greater than the problems encountered in the mechanical harvesting of small grains.

To be of any consequence new knowledge must be put to use. Not only the rate of invention but also the rate of diffusion of new ideas is crucial in determining the rate at which productivity can advance. In the post-Civil War era three important avenues of diffusion were available: printed material, word of mouth, and the embodiment of new ideas in new capital goods. Farmers could obtain printed information from an extensive rural press, from the reports of state agricultural societies, and from the publications of the Department of Agriculture and the state experiment stations. Probably only a small fraction of all farmers ever read these sources of information. Those who did, however, were typically the relatively wealthy, large landowners who were more inclined toward systematic experimentation. They were the leaders in their communities,

Bulletin of the Oxford University Institute of Economics and Statistics, XXVI (Feb. 1964), 69–70.

and their successful experiments were readily observed and imitated by others who might never have obtained information directly from the published sources. It seems certain that the most extensive avenue for the transmission of information in the countryside was simply word of mouth. Farmers talked of farming with one another—over the fence, at the general store, after the sermon on Sunday. Even Grange meetings, so often considered from a political point of view, might well have been more important as vehicles for the dissemination of technical and economic information. County and state fairs performed a similar function.

Competition among machinery manufacturers led them to embody new ideas in their equipment, and their ubiquitous salesmen were quick to bring such advances to the attention of farmers. Since the embodiment of new ideas in farm machinery was an important avenue of diffusion for technological advances, the rate of productivity increase was indirectly as well as directly tied to the accumulation of material capital. Figure 4.8 shows that a close correspondence did exist between the rate of advance of output per worker and the rate of increase of material capital per worker. Such evidence is very crude and bears only indirectly on the embodiment hypothesis; nevertheless, the available data are consistent with the hypothesis.

V

GROWTH AND INEQUALITY

> [W]hatever disadvantage or detriment the introduction and use of new and improved instrumentalities or methods of production and distribution may temporarily entail on individuals or classes, the ultimate result is always an almost immeasurable degree of increased good to mankind in general. [However] That many of the features of the situation are, when considered by themselves, disagreeable and even appalling, can not be denied.
>
> DAVID A. WELLS

REGIONAL DISPARITIES IN DEVELOPMENT

Generalizations concerning the entire United States must often be qualified to take into account substantial differences among regions; such was the case in our discussions of population growth, urbanization, and agricultural development. Personal income per capita, a crude measure of the average level of material well-being, also differed markedly in the various parts of the nation. Among contemporaries these differences sometimes gave rise to political antagonism, and "sectional" issues play a large part in American political history. In 1880, the first year within the post-Civil War era for which state income data are available, estimated personal income per capita varied from a low of $46 in North Carolina to a high of $318 in Nevada. Southern states generally had income levels of about half the national average; some Western states had income levels more than twice the national average; and other states varied between these extremes (Table 5.1).

TABLE 5.1
REGIONAL PERSONAL INCOME PER CAPITA
RELATIVE TO THE NATIONAL AVERAGE
(NATIONAL AVERAGE = 100)

Regions	1880	1900	1920
Northeast	141	137	132
New England	141	134	124
Middle Atlantic	141	139	134
North Central	98	103	100
East North Central	102	106	108
West North Central	90	97	87
South	51	51	62
South Atlantic	45	45	59
East South Central	51	49	52
West South Central	60	61	72
West	190	154	122
Mountain	168	139	100
Pacific	204	163	135

SOURCE. Richard A. Easterlin, "Regional Income Trends, 1840–1950," in Seymour E. Harris, Ed., *American Economic History* (New York: McGraw-Hill, 1961), p. 528. Regions are defined as in Table 2.8. The relative income of 163 for the West in 1900, which is given in the above source, is in error. The figure given here, 154, is computed from data shown in Richard A. Easterlin, "Interregional Differences in Per Capita Income, Population, and Total Income, 1840–1950," in National Bureau of Economic Research, Conference on Research in Income and Wealth, *Trends in the American Economy in the Nineteenth Century* (Princeton, N. J.: Princeton University, 1960), p. 137.

Southern income levels remained substantially below those elsewhere throughout the post-Civil War era, but scholars have too often exaggerated the problems of Southern development. Statistics themselves—it would be more accurate to say *naively interpreted* statistics—are partly to blame for a fascination with Southern "backwardness" and "stagnation." Money wage levels, for example, were typically lower in the South than elsewhere; but because the prices of consumer goods were also typically lower, the gap between *real wages* in the South and elsewhere was less than simple comparisons of money wage figures would indicate. Correction for the relatively high prices of the Far West, it might be added, would substantially reduce the relative incomes of that area. Even when we make such corrections, however, it remains true that Southern earnings on the average fell below those elsewhere. No special theory of "Southern backwardness" is required to explain this differential; indeed, it can be explained by a general theory that accounts for differences of income levels among *all* the regions.

Economic theory asserts that output (or income) per worker differs among regions because of differences in the amounts of material, human, and intellectual capital—inputs that are generally highly correlated with one another—each worker has to assist him in production. As we saw when investigating agricultural output per worker in the various regions, the crude and indirect evidence that exists is consistent with this hypothesis. Although we lack the kind of data that would permit a direct test of the more general hypothesis concerning regional income differentials, a variety of indirect evidence is consistent with it. One study found that among the states in 1919, wages per worker and material capital per worker in manufacturing were significantly related.[1] Many studies of more recent periods have discovered such a significant relation, which causes us to suspect that the relation also existed in the earlier period. We emphasize again, however, that such evidence is consistent with the hypothesis only under the assumption that the three kinds of capital accumulation are highly correlated.

Investment in formal education was closely related to the level of income per capita. Notably, the cluster of states in the lower left corner of Figure 5.1, a position indicating both relatively low investment in formal education and relatively low income, consists of the 11 states of the Confederacy plus Kentucky and West Virginia; the lowest ranking non-Southern state exceeds the highest ranking Southern state in both dimensions of the figure. The relation also obtained among the non-Southern states, with the exception of two frontier mining states, Nevada and Colorado, for which the divergencies have an obvious explanation. Of course, the correlation portrayed in the figure does nothing to establish the direction of causality, but it is consistent with the hypothesis that relatively small investments in human capital contributed toward relatively low per capita incomes among the various states.

Between 1880 and 1900, income per capita increased as rapidly in the South as in the non-South, while Western incomes grew substantially slower and Northeastern incomes slightly slower than the national average (Table 5.1). Contrary to assertions of Southern "stagnation" in the post-Civil War era, the South did not lag behind the rest of the nation after 1880. Of course, even though its rate of growth was equal to the national average, the *absolute* difference between Southern and non-Southern in-

[1] Harvey S. Perloff, *et al., Regions, Resources, and Economic Growth* (Baltimore: Johns Hopkins, 1960), p. 579. The simple coefficient of correlation between wages per worker and capital per worker is 0.63, a level that could have been produced by pure chance less than one time in a thousand experiments.

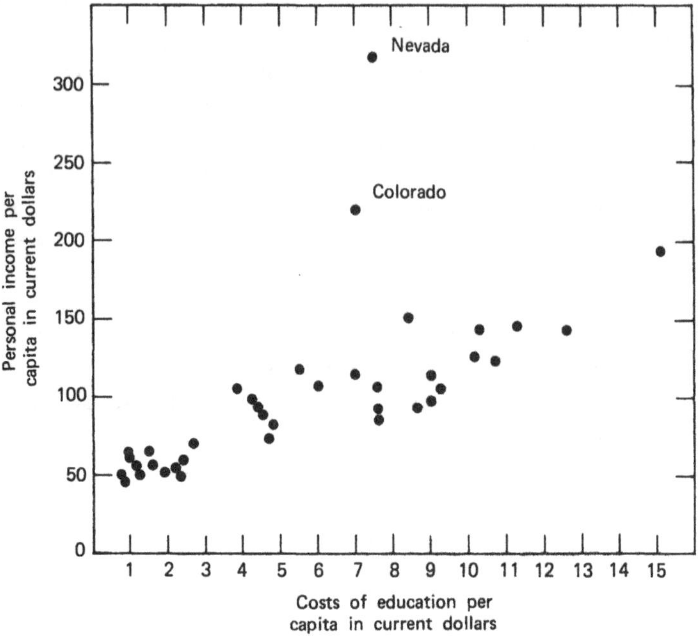

Figure 5.1 Relation between income and investment in formal education, by states, 1880. *Source:* Lewis C. Solmon, "Estimates of the Costs of Schooling in 1880 and 1890," *Explorations in Economic History,* VII (Supplement; 1970), 534.

come levels became wider. Perhaps this is the gap that historians and other observers have had in mind when discussing the increasing "backwardness" of the South. Regional groupings obscure substantial differences among the individual states, but the dispersion of the states around the national average level of income did become somewhat smaller during the two decades after 1880. Between the turn of the century and 1920 the South made large gains, while the Northeast and the West again sustained losses relative to the national average. Overall, the four decades after 1880 witnessed a relative narrowing of regional differences in personal income per capita.

How can this narrowing be explained? A theory to answer this question is a simple extension of the theory employed to explain regional differences at a point in time. At any given time in the post-Civil War era the resource endowment of any region differed from that of other regions. For example, the West possessed relatively large quantities of land, the Northeast relatively large quantities of all kinds of capital except land, and the South relatively large quantities of unskilled labor. The resource that was relatively most abundant in a region commanded a relatively low rate of return. For instance, unskilled laborers in Alabama, where they were relatively abundant, earned a lower real wage than they did in California, where they were relatively scarce. Resource owners sought to obtain higher returns by moving their resources—whether labor or some form of capital—to areas characterized by a relative scarcity of that resource. Workers migrated to places where they could obtain higher real wages, and capitalists sought to invest in areas promising the highest rate of return, as we have already seen in the discussion of farm mortgage lending.[2] If underlying economic conditions had remained unchanged, such movements would eventually have resulted in an approximate equalization of returns among all regions for each kind of resource. But of course the world did not stand still. Before a complete adjustment had been made, new changes occurred in demand and technology, upsetting the old pattern of adjustment. In practice, therefore, the interregional transfer of resources produced only a tendency toward equalization of returns, never an actual realization of equality. Moreover, some of the adjustments occurred at a snail's pace, so divergencies persisted throughout the period, especially when the causes of the original divergencies were self-reinforcing. The same differentials among returns that gave rise to interregional migration of resources also encouraged individuals within each of the regions to accumulate that form of capital being attracted from other areas. Together the accumulation of capital within regions and the transfer of resources among regions produced the tendency toward equalization.

What we know about the movement of resources in the post-Civil War era is broadly consistent with the hypothesis just sketched. Net in-migration relative to population was largest in the West and substantially lower in the Northeast and Great Lakes regions; and in the South the number of out-migrants exceeded the number of in-migrants in every decade of the period. Eastern capitalists did transfer their resources to the South and the West more frequently than the reverse occurred. With workers moving into areas of relative labor scarcity and capital into areas of relative capital scarcity, the ratio of capital to labor drew closer to equality among the regions, and a narrowing of interregional income differentials was the consequence. That differences remained is attributable to deficiencies of information about opportunities elsewhere, to costs of transferring resources, to difficulties in borrowing to finance the trans-

2 Actually, resource transfer is attractive only when the present value of the expected gains obtainable by the transfer exceeds the costs of the transfer; the migration of resources should be considered in the same terms as any other investment. In the present discussion we are abstracting from the costs of the transfer.

fer, and to continuing disturbances in the economy that altered the distribution of opportunities among the regions and changed the desirable pattern of adjustments.

It is curious that historians have often condemned the capital movements among regions as harmful to the areas receiving the capital. The distinguished historian of the South, C. Vann Woodward, for example, refers again and again to the "heedless exploitation of Southern resources and people by Northeastern capital."[3] This interpretation is simply wrong. Surely any reasonable definition of "exploitation"—though this value-laden word would be better abandoned than defined—requires that an "exploited" region be worse off than it would be if left "unexploited." But the transfer of Northeastern resources into the South certainly did not make that region worse off; rather, the reverse was true. Even had the owners of the capital removed *all* their earnings from the region—which they did not—the South would still have benefited from the increased demand for local labor and materials, the expanded tax base, and all the benefits attributable to the new activities for which the owners could not charge—for example, the learning from experience gained by their employees. Interregional transfers of resources occurred through free contracting among the parties involved; that individuals voluntarily arranged the transfer suggests that each side considered the arrangement to its own advantage.

Underlying the claims of regional "exploitation" seem frequently to be the implicit assumptions that all regions "should" be equally industrialized and that while manufacturing is a Good Thing, agriculture and mining are activities fit only for slaves and other "exploited" people. Such views make no sense. The people of any region can maximize their incomes by pursuing the activities that make relatively intensive use of resources that are relatively abundant, and hence relatively cheap, in that region. To pursue other activities would be to sacrifice the benefits of specialization and trade. It is obvious that given the resource endowments of their regions, the advantage of Southerners and Westerners lay mainly in agriculture and other extractive industries, while Northeasterners stood to gain by concentrating on manufacturing and other nonagricultural activities. No one had to dictate these patterns of specialization, and no one did. The rate of return on the various activities attempted in the different regions provided a signal, informing entrepreneurs of the ways in which they, and therefore their regions, could obtain the highest possible incomes.

If we agree that interregional differences in income per capita re-

[3] C. Vann Woodward, *Origins of the New South, 1877–1913* (n. p.: Louisiana State University, 1951), p. 473.

sulted from differences in the capital/labor ratio and that during the 1880–1920 period the South actually gained on the rest of the nation, the really crucial question becomes: why was the capital/labor ratio relatively so low in the South in 1880? How could one region fall so far out of line with the others in an economy of mobile—though not costlessly mobile—resources? To answer this question requires a digression to consider the prewar economy.

Before the Civil War, slaves lacked property rights of any kind. Moreover, they *were* property, the most important form of Southern capital except land. In applying economic theory to predict the decisions of investors before the war, we must consider slaves in the same terms as machines, land, or inventories, simply as a form of capital. Under such circumstances economic theory predicts that the interregional flow of resources would tend to equalize only the incomes per capita *of the free population* of each region. And indeed the evidence is consistent with this prediction. Richard Easterlin found that in 1840, "if the slaves and their income (estimated at subsistence) are eliminated, one finds that the income of the white population in the South exceeded the national average and compared favorably with that of the Northeast."[4] Because Southern incomes grew somewhat more rapidly than the national average during the two decades before the Civil War, the level of Southern personal income per white capita exceeded the national average even more in 1860.[5]

The emancipation had two important effects. First, it destroyed part of the assets owned by the whites by outlawing their property rights in slaves; second, it added about four million persons to the Southern free population. Emancipation in no way affected the stock of *real resources* in the South; from a social point of view it destroyed nothing. In effect, it merely relabeled "machines" as "citizens" and gave them property rights to match their new status. (That the actual rights of blacks turned out to be more restricted than those of whites does not affect the present argument.) This change raises insurmountable problems of intertemporal comparison. To compare the level of income *per free capita* in 1860 with the same measure for a postwar year makes no sense; but neither does a comparison of incomes per capita of the *total* population when a third of that population consisted of "machines" at the first date. *Per capita incomes at the two dates simply are not comparable in any meaningful sense.* The emancipation in a single stroke increased the denominator of the fraction (income/free population) by transforming part of the

[4] Richard A. Easterlin, "Regional Income Trends, 1840–1950," in Seymour E. Harris, Ed., *American Economic History* (New York: McGraw-Hill, 1961), p. 527.

[5] Stanley L. Engerman, "The Economic Impact of the Civil War," *Explorations in Entrepreneurial History,* III (Spring/Summer 1966), 194, n. 20.

capital stock into part of the population. Of course the level of income per free capita then dramatically declined, quite apart from the vast wartime destruction of Southern human and material capital. By a revolutionary restructuring of property rights the emancipation created a completely different set of feasible opportunities from the investor's point of view, changing the slave owner's valuable asset into the body of a new citizen. In this new legal framework investors, including now the freedmen, groped toward an adjustment, channeling their investments into those avenues—including migration—promising the highest rate of return. But we would hardly expect the achievement of a new equilibrium to occur immediately. The blow to the Southern *asset structure* was too disturbing for Southerners to adjust to quickly; in the economist's jargon, the emancipation created a massive "portfolio disequilibrium." In addition, postwar conditions did little to assist and much to retard a new adjustment.[6] In retrospect, it is perhaps most remarkable that the Southern economy managed to rebound as quickly as it did.

A major implication of the preceding arguments deserves to be emphasized. The decline of Southern incomes below the national average is entirely attributable to the Civil War and its effects, and the region has been catching up ever since. The relative poverty of the South in the post-Civil War era—and indeed right up to the present day—is therefore entirely attributable to (1) the existence of the slave system and (2) the abolition of that system through destructive civil war and haphazard emancipation. Moralists might well hold Southerners accountable for the first, but hardly for the second. How ironic that the Great Emancipator should have engineered a policy that has kept Southerners, black and white alike, relatively poor for over a century. To be sure, the Union was saved, but only at such great and enduring cost. Had Americans been able in 1860 to foresee the future, it seems likely that a fully compensated, carefully organized emancipation would have appealed more strongly to both Northerners and Southerners.

IMMIGRANTS AND "EXPLOITATION"

The people who left their European homes in search of better opportunities in the United States typically discovered something less than the

[6] In particular, the National Banking Act, passed during the Civil War, did much to retard Southern recovery. See Richard Sylla, "Federal Policy, Banking Market Structure, and Capital Mobilization in the United States, 1863–1913," *Journal of Economic History,* XXIX (Dec. 1969).

Promised Land. In 1890 Jacob Riis gave a classic account of their living conditions in the slums of New York City, the major receiving center. There the Jewish child, only recently arrived from Poland, "works unchallenged from the day he is old enough to pull a thread. There is no such thing as a dinner hour; men and women eat while they work, and the 'day' is lengthened at both ends far into the night. Factory hands take their work with them at the close of the lawful day to eke out their scanty earnings by working overtime at home." Not far away Riis found the Bohemians suffering from what seemed to him "a slavery as real as any that ever disgraced the South."[7] And he went on to record in heartrending detail the long hours and meager earnings of other recently arrived immigrant groups. Such facts have led a distinguished historian of immigration to conclude: "The immigrant was an exploited unskilled laborer."[8] And this interpretation seems standard in the historical literature.

Riis accurately, if somewhat overdramatically, described what he saw. But his observations, the basis for so many subsequent accounts of living conditions among the immigrants, were not representative; in fact, they were systematically biased. His main interest was in improving living conditions within the tenement districts, and it is hardly surprising that in his visits to the slums he observed immigrants who were mostly poor, some of them desperately so. However, not all immigrants lived in the slums, nor were they uniformly destitute. As Table 5.2 shows, the earnings of immigrant workers actually varied widely. Just as regional differences make it hazardous to generalize about the entire United States, so differences among the various immigrant groups make it hazardous to generalize about "the" immigrant. But this variation itself raises an obvious question: how can differences in earnings among the various immigrant groups be explained? We shall see that an answer to this question also leads directly to an explanation of why each group "came in at the bottom of the economic ladder" and how each subsequently "worked its way up."

Scholars have advanced two alternative hypotheses to explain variations in earnings among immigrant ethnic groups. The first is that the groups possessed on the average different amounts of useful skills, and therefore their labor services commanded different earnings in the marketplace. The second maintains that ethnic prejudice against immigrants from southern and eastern Europe resulted in discrimination against them in the labor market, depressing their earnings below the level of

[7] Jacob Riis, *How the Other Half Lives* (New York: Charles Scribner's Sons, 1890), pp. 123–24, 136.

[8] Oscar Handlin, *The Uprooted* (Boston: Little, Brown and Company, 1952), p. 195.

TABLE 5.2

CHARACTERISTICS OF ADULT, MALE, FOREIGN-BORN WORKERS IN MINING AND MANUFACTURING OCCUPATIONS, 1909

Group	Number Reporting Earnings	Average Weekly Earnings in Dollars	Percentage Speaking English	Percentage Literate	Percentage Residing in U.S. 5 Years or More
Armenian	594	9.73	54.9	92.1	54.6
Bohemian and Moravian	1,353	13.07	66.0	96.8	71.2
Bulgarian	403	10.31	20.3	78.2	8.5
Canadian, French	8,164	10.62	79.4	84.1	86.7
Canadian, other	1,323	14.15	100.0	99.0	90.8
Croatian	4,890	11.37	50.9	70.7	38.9
Danish	377	14.32	96.5	99.2	85.4
Dutch	1,026	12.04	86.1	97.9	81.9
English	9,408	14.13	100.0	98.9	80.6
Finnish	3,334	13.27	50.3	99.1	53.6
Flemish	125	11.07	45.6	92.1	32.9
French	896	12.92	68.6	94.3	70.1
German	11,380	13.63	87.5	98.0	86.4
Greek	4,154	8.41	33.5	84.2	18.0
Hebrew, Russian	3,177	12.71	74.7	93.3	57.1
Hebrew, other	1,158	14.37	79.5	92.8	73.8
Irish	7,596	13.01	100.0	96.0	90.6
Italian, north	5,343	11.28	58.8	85.0	55.2

equally skilled native-born workers or immigrants from northwestern Europe. The second hypothesis often takes the form of claims that certain immigrant groups were "exploited."

To test the hypothesis of skill differentials, a recent study employed the data shown in Table 5.2.[9] Literacy and the ability to speak English serve as indexes of skill. The study found that the relation between earnings, ability to speak English, and literacy is best represented by the equation

[9] Robert Higgs, "Race, Skills, and Earnings: American Immigrants in 1909," *Journal of Economic History*, XXXI (June 1971). This paper contains an assessment of the data shown in Table 5.2; it also presents the technical features of the statistical results summarized below and a more detailed discussion of the problems examined in this section.

TABLE 5.2 (*Continued*)

Group	Number Reporting Earnings	Average Weekly Earnings in Dollars	Percentage Speaking English	Percentage Literate	Percentage Residing in U.S. 5 Years or More
Italian, south	7,821	9.61	48.7	69.3	47.8
Lithuanian	4,661	11.03	51.3	78.5	53.8
Macedonian	479	8.95	21.1	69.4	2.0
Magyar	5,331	11.65	46.4	90.9	44.1
Norwegian	420	15.28	96.9	99.7	79.3
Polish	24,223	11.06	43.5	80.1	54.1
Portuguese	3,125	8.10	45.2	47.8	57.5
Roumanian	1,026	10.90	33.3	83.3	12.0
Russian	3,311	11.01	43.6	74.6	38.0
Ruthenian	385	9.92	36.8	65.9	39.6
Scotch	1,711	15.24	100.0	99.6	83.6
Servian	1,016	10.75	41.2	71.5	31.4
Slovak	10,775	11.95	55.6	84.5	60.0
Slovenian	2,334	12.15	51.7	87.3	49.9
Swedish	3,984	15.36	94.7	99.8	87.4
Syrian	812	8.12	54.6	75.1	45.3
Turkish	240	7.65	22.5	56.5	10.0

SOURCE. U. S. Immigration Commission, *Report* (Washington: Government Printing Office, 1911), I, pp. 367, 474, 439, 352. In this table, "literate" means able to read.

$$Y = 2.55 + 0.0383E + 0.0796L$$

where Y is a group's weekly average earnings in dollars, E is the percentage of a group speaking English, and L is the percentage of a group literate in any language. The equation can be interpreted as follows: holding the level of literacy constant, a 10-percentage-point increase in the proportion of a group speaking English was associated with an increase of about 38 cents per week in the group's average earnings; holding the level of English-speaking constant, a 10-percentage-point increase in the proportion of a group literate was associated with an increase of almost 80 cents per week in the group's average earnings. Each of these partial relations is statistically significant—could have been produced by pure chance less than one time in a hundred experiments—which means that the data are consistent with the hypothesis of skill differentials leading to earnings differentials. The overall relation statistically "explains" almost four fifths of the variance among the earnings of the groups; in statistical jargon, the equation provides a good "fit" for the data.

The Immigration Commission, which obtained the data shown in Table 5.2, also collected information from 41,933 native-born white employees in manufacturing and mining occupations to obtain a control group for its study of immigrants. The average earnings of these workers, all of whom spoke English and 98.2 percent of whom were literate, was $14.37 per week. To test the hypothesis that immigrants were the objects of ethnic discrimination, we use the equation relating skills to earnings among immigrants to predict the earnings of the native-born workers. If employers actually discriminated against immigrants, such a prediction would fall significantly below the actual earnings of the native-born workers. Remarkably, the prediction falls only 1 percent below the actual figure, a result that casts grave doubt on the notion that ethnic discrimination operated on a wide scale to the detriment of immigrant workers.[10]

This finding does *not* mean that no ethnic prejudice existed, and there is plenty of evidence that such prejudice did exist. But it is apparent that if some (discriminating) employers offered the immigrant a wage lower than the actual value of his labor services to the firm, another employer could increase his wealth by hiring that employee at a slightly higher wage. Of course, with many employers, each attempting to maximize wealth, competition for workers would soon force the wage up to a level at which it equalled the actual value of the worker's labor services to the firm. Not every employer must be a wealth maximizer to obtain this result, however. In principle, just *one* would be enough, for it would pay him to outbid other (discriminating) employers for labor and to expand his business as long as he could continue to obtain workers at less than the going rate for equally skilled native-born workers. The evidence is quite convincing that at least some employers in the post-Civil War era strongly preferred wealth to the pleasures of discrimination. (Notice that our argument is just the reverse of the common belief that discrimination allows the employer to increase his wealth by "exploiting" his workers; this popular fallacy fails to take competition for labor into consideration.)[11]

From these findings it is only a short step to an explanation of why each new immigrant group "came in at the bottom of the economic

[10] The predicted earnings figure is $2.55 + 0.0383\ (100.0) + 0.0796\ (98.2) = 14.20$.

[11] For a complete discussion of the theory summarized in this paragraph, see Gary S. Becker, *The Economics of Discrimination* (Chicago: University of Chicago, 1957), especially pp. 35–37.

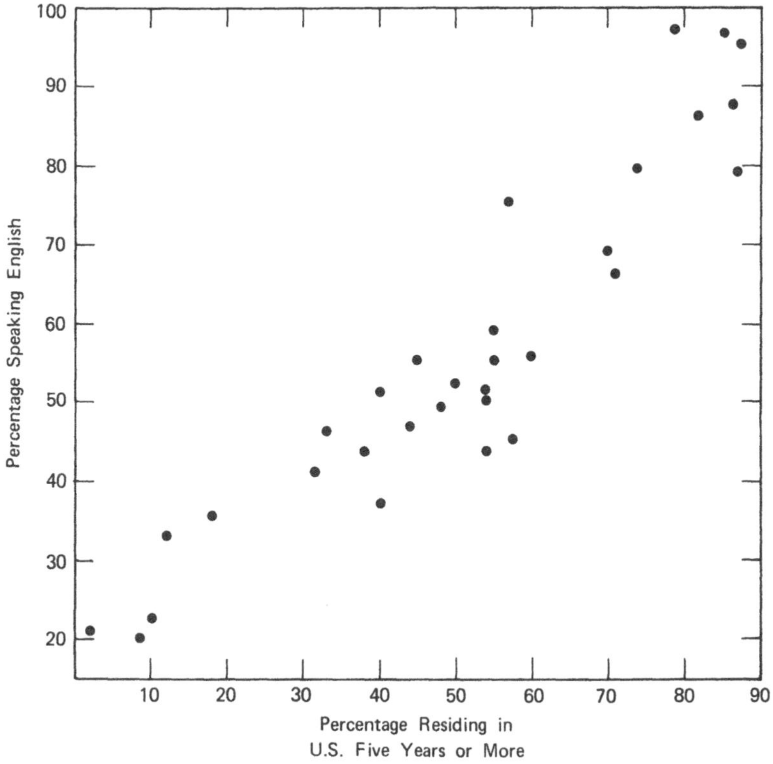

Figure 5.2 Relation between ability to speak English and length of residence in U. S., 31 non-English-speaking ethnic groups, 1909. *Source:* Table 5.2 above.

ladder." It was partly because later groups were upon arrival less literate, which probably implies less skilled generally, than those having resided longer in the United States, and partly because they had less command of English. The ability to speak English was almost perfectly correlated with the duration of a group's residence in America (Figure 5.2)—a good example of learning from experience, since few of these men ever received formal instruction in the English language. Over time the immigrants gained fluency in English and other skills, and in the process their earnings rose; those arriving later merely followed in the footsteps of those arriving earlier, and ethnic discrimination had little or no effect on the process. At any point in time, however, different groups occupied different positions on the ladder of skill acquisition, and hence correspondingly different positions on the earnings scale.

INEQUALITIES BETWEEN WHITES AND BLACKS

Inequalities between whites and blacks apparently existed in virtually all aspects of social and economic life throughout the post-Civil War era. Beyond this sweeping and obvious statement, however, very little can be said, for economic historians have just begun to study trends in racial inequalities during this period, and reliable findings have yet to appear. The absolute well-being of blacks certainly improved to some extent during the half century after the Civil War; the extremely low starting point, if nothing else, made some gains almost inevitable. Thousands of blacks migrated to regions of greater opportunity; a substantial majority learned to read and write; and many acquired land and other property—all of which worked to raise black incomes. Whether the rate of growth of black incomes exceeded the rate of growth of white incomes, however, remains open to conjecture. Given this dearth of knowledge, our discussion in this section can do little more than lay the groundwork for research that remains to be done.

Lacking income or earnings statistics, Gary Becker in his study of discrimination constructed an index of occupational standing for male blacks relative to male whites in nonfarm occupations in 1910. This index stood at 73 percent in the North and 67 percent in the South.[12] A similar but more detailed and inclusive index constructed by Dale L. Hiestand stood at 78 percent for the entire nation in 1910.[13] Unfortunately, however, the type of index constructed by Becker and Hiestand is biased upward as an indicator of relative earnings, for it assumes that the only difference between the races lay in their distribution among the various occupations—the index being less than unity because blacks were more concentrated in the lower-paying jobs. But a second source of differences in earnings, not captured by this index, is that within a particular job classification blacks typically earned less than whites. Moreover, blacks may have been more frequently unemployed. Clearly, indexes of relative occupational standing are open to serious objections, and in any event earlier observations are required before we can reach any conclusions about trends in the half century after the emancipation.

Any discussion of inequalities between whites and blacks in the post-

[12] *Ibid.*, p. 113.

[13] Dale L. Hiestand, "The Changing Position of Negro Workers," in John F. Kain, Ed., *Race and Poverty* (Englewood Cliffs, N. J.: Prentice-Hall, 1969), p. 72.

Civil War era must take slavery as its point of departure. Under that system, slave owners had an interest in maintaining slaves at a level of well-being that would preserve their physical vitality, but beyond that level any outlays were wasted. Consequently, slaves existed at approximately the level of a physical subsistence income. Upon emancipation, blacks found themselves with few skills, without physical property, and concentrated in the devastated South. In the following half century they discovered that despite Constitutional amendments and civil-rights laws they had yet to attain full rights of citizenship. Lynch law took its toll in deaths and intimidation; many states devised ways of limiting black access to the polls; and white-dominated courts dealt out something less than equal justice. In effect, blacks labored under insecure civil liberties and uncertain private property rights, and this kind of "official" oppression constituted much more of an obstacle to their economic progress than discrimination against them in the market, though that also existed.

At any time in the past century, black earnings fall considerably below those of whites. This fact alone, however, implies nothing about racial discrimination in the labor market. To determine whether racial discrimination exists, we must be careful to compare workers identical in every respect except race, for even without racial discrimination, earnings differentials might exist because of differentials in age, sex, education, health, and other "productivity factors." If earnings differentials remain after adjustment for productivity factors, the evidence is consistent with the hypothesis of purely racial discrimination.[14] It is true, of course, that even if no discrimination exists in the labor market, earnings differentials could still be ascribed to discrimination if blacks are denied equal access to education or equal treatment under the law. Thus, discrimination may exist at two levels—in both the market and nonmarket sectors of resource allocation—and it is important to distinguish between them.

In the section above on "Immigrants and 'Exploitation'," we found that among immigrant groups in 1909, earnings and skills were closely related. We saw too that the earnings-skills relation gave an accurate prediction of the earnings of native-born white workers of comparable age, sex, and industrial affiliation. The Immigration Commission, which obtained the data used in our earlier tests, also collected comparable information from 6604 adult, native-born black males employed in mining and manufacturing industries in 1909. The workers in this sample earned an average of $10.66 per week. As a crude test of the racial discrimination hypothesis, we can use the earnings-skills relation presented in the pre-

[14] For an example of a study that makes such adjustments, employing data for 1960, see James D. Gwartney, "Discrimination and Income Differentials," *American Economic Review*, LX (June 1970).

vious section to predict the earnings of the black workers. If racial discrimination existed, the predicted earnings should significantly exceed actual earnings. In fact, the earnings predicted for this sample of black workers, all of whom spoke English and 76.4 percent of whom were literate, stands $1.80 above their actual earnings—a finding consistent with the hypothesis of racial discrimination, though a very crude finding to be sure.[15]

To say something more definite about the extent of labor market discrimination against black workers, we must obtain more detailed information on earnings and skills. Table 5.3 presents some crude industry

TABLE 5.3

EARNINGS, LITERACY, AND AGE OF BLACKS RELATIVE TO WHITES, ADULT MALE EMPLOYEES, 1909

Industry	Relative Mean Earnings	Relative Proportion Literate	Relative Mean Age
Agricultural implements and vehicles	0.86	0.93	1.09
Cigars and tobacco	0.62	0.80	1.04
Bituminous coal mining	0.86	0.78	1.03
Construction	0.74	0.75	0.92
Glass	0.72	0.86	1.09
Iron and steel	0.64	0.76	1.00
Iron ore mining	0.92	0.62	1.04
Meatpacking	0.93	0.95	0.98

SOURCE. Calculated from data in U. S. Immigration Commission, *Report* (Washington: Government Printing Office, 1911), XX, pp. 227–28, 270–71, 581, 1068–69.

data obtained from the report of the Immigration Commission. These data indicate no apparent relation between relative earnings and relative literacy or age, a finding that suggests that the earnings differentials may have been partly determined by discrimination. For the eight industries as a whole, however, black literacy does fall below white literacy in roughly the same proportion as earnings fall short. Still, these data are much too crude and too few to support any firm conclusions.

The evidence considered in this section illustrates some of the difficulties in historical studies of racial discrimination. Perhaps, too, it can serve as a warning against drawing quick conclusions about a subject that engages strong emotions but remains little explored by scientific re-

[15] The predicted earnings figure is $2.55 + 0.0383\ (100.0) + 0.0796\ (76.4) = 12.46$.

search. At present we can do little more than offer some conjectures for consideration in future studies. First, all existing evidence indicates more intense discrimination in the South than in the North. This fact suggests that a major determinant of the relative economic position of blacks has been their regional distribution. We need to know much more about what variables determined the rate and direction of black migrations, both interregionally and within the South. Second, differences between the economic progress of European immigrants and of blacks suggest three major hypotheses: that blacks began to accumulate skills from a much lower starting point than the immigrants; that blacks experienced greater discrimination than immigrants in the nonmarket sector, especially in obtaining education and equal treatment under the law; or that ethnic prejudice against blacks in the labor market was more intense and widespread than that against immigrants. Combinations of these hypotheses are of course possible. Third, discrimination against blacks in the market often depended on discrimination in the nonmarket sector, as, for example, when Southern white employers who strongly preferred wealth to discrimination, and would have bid up black wages, were illegally intimidated by fellow whites intent on keeping the black "in his place." We need to know much more about the relation between the market and the nonmarket varieties of discrimination and about the enforcement techniques employed within the white community to maintain effective discrimination.

WAS PROGRESS WORTH ITS PRICE?

A comparison of the American economy in 1865 with the economy in 1914 points up a variety of changes. On the eve of the Great War Americans consumed about three times more economic goods per capita than they had a half century earlier. They lived longer and healthier lives and spent less time at work and more at recreation. They were better housed and educated, traveled more, read more, and were better informed about their own and other countries. All of this we customarily call Progress.

Against the gains of economic growth, however, must be set the costs of realizing the gains. Economic growth was an inherently disruptive process, and because certainty itself is an economic good, unanticipated disruptions constituted one of the costs of growth. Business depressions erratically punctuated the course of growth, leaving workers without jobs and employers with losses, but in an unregulated market economy such fluctuations were both unavoidable and unpredictable (Table 5.4).

TABLE 5.4
ESTIMATED PERCENTAGE OF LABOR FORCE UNEMPLOYED IN SELECTED DEPRESSION YEARS

Year	Percentage Unemployed
1876	12–14
1885	6–8
1894	18
1908	8

SOURCE. Stanley Lebergott, *Manpower in Economic Growth* (New York: McGraw-Hill, 1964), pp. 187, 512, 522.

Though inventions led to increased efficiency in production, they often meant bankruptcy for those employing older processes. David A. Wells, despite his pervasive optimism, was perceptive enough to recognize that "nothing marks more clearly the rate of material progress than the rapidity with which that which is old and has been considered wealth is destroyed by the results of new inventions and discoveries."[16] Though migration allowed young people to obtain higher incomes, it often left their parents lonely and unhappy in the old home. Though the settlement of fertile Western lands provided cheaper food for urban dwellers, it often meant ruin for Eastern farmers. And similar contrasts might be recited at great length. We could say that people did adjust; ultimately everyone was better off. But such an interpretation is incomplete and ignores the costs imposed on people by the disruptive transformations that inevitably accompanied economic growth.

The inescapable fact is that economic growth hurt many people. Some recovered their losses, but others did not. Economic growth meant Progress from a social point of view because it created more wealth than it destroyed, but the distribution of the gains and losses was quite unequal. If we are interested in individual welfare, the answer to the question "Was progress worth its price?" must necessarily be that for some it was, and for others it was not. It will hardly do to say that individuals "freely chose to have economic growth," because growth was a social process; the actions of a single individual simply did not matter one way or the other. An individual could determine his own program of saving and investment, but he could neither foresee nor control the future development of the market system. He could not know that the investments made in such hopeful expectations and based on the most reliable available information were often destined to become reductions in his wealth.

[16] David A. Wells, *Recent Economic Changes* (New York: Appleton, 1889), p. 31.

American society encouraged economic growth by guaranteeing individuals secure private property rights and free access to markets, but the specification of property rights did not permit all economic actions and their effects to be determined through free contracting. In the absence of all-embracing rights of contract—an impossibility in any event—many external or "spillover" effects were inevitable, some of them beneficial but others quite harmful. The Supreme Court clearly recognized the problem in deciding the case of *Coppage v. Kansas* (1915):

> No doubt, wherever the right of private property exists, there must and will be inequalities of fortune; and thus it naturally happens that parties negotiating about a contract are not equally unhampered by circumstances. . . . Since it is self-evident that unless all things are held in common, some persons must have more property than others, it is from the nature of things impossible to uphold freedom of contract and the right to private property without at the same time recognizing as legitimate those inequalities of fortune that are the necessary result of the exercise of those rights.[17]

By not holding people liable for all the effects of all their actions, American society widened the scope of free individual actions, but at the same time it forfeited the kind of security and order that can exist in a stationary economy. In a free market economy the race was to the swift—and, of course, to the lucky, for even the swift sometimes ran in the wrong direction.

[17] Cited in John R. Commons, *Legal Foundations of Capitalism* (New York: Macmillan, 1924), p. 291.

APPENDIX: The Sources of Economic Growth

This appendix explains the derivation of the conclusions presented in Chapter II concerning the sources of economic growth for the period 1869–1914.

The basic assumptions are that the economy has an aggregate production function characterized by constant returns to scale and that all markets are in competitive equilibrium. Given these assumptions, the production function can be written as

$$(1) \qquad Y = A\, K^{\alpha}\, L^{1-\alpha}$$

where Y = total output, A = index of total input productivity, K = material capital stock (including land), L = man-hours worked, and α = share of property owners in total income. By taking logarithms and then differentiating with respect to time, we can express (1) as

$$(2) \qquad Y' = A' + \alpha K' + (1-\alpha) L'$$

where primes denote proportional rates of change. This states that the rate of growth of total output is the sum of the rates of growth of total input productivity, labor, and material capital, where the growth rates of the inputs are weighted by their relative income shares.

By subtracting L' from each side of (2), we obtain

$$(3) \qquad y' = A' + \alpha k'$$

where y = output per man-hour and k = ratio of material capital to labor. This states that the rate of growth of output per man-hour is the sum of the rate of growth of total input productivity and the weighted rate of growth of the material capital intensity, where the weight is the property share of income.

From data given in John W. Kendrick, *Productivity Trends in the United States* (Princeton, N. J.: Princeton University, 1961), pp. 298–99, 311–12, and 320–21, we obtain the following growth rates for the period 1869–1914: $Y' = 4.2$ percent per year; $L' = 2.5$ percent per year; and $K' = 3.9$ percent per year. From data given in Edward C. Budd, "Factor Shares, 1850–1910," in National Bureau of Economic Research, Conference on Research in Income and Wealth, *Trends in the American Economy in the Nineteenth Century* (Princeton, N. J.: Princeton University, 1960), p. 387, it appears that the relative income shares were approximately constant during the period at $\alpha = 1/3$. Substituting these data in (2), A' can be calculated, and therefore the proportional influence of three broad sources of growth in total output obtained as follows: the increase in man-hours accounts for $1.67/4.20 = 40$ percent; the growth of material capital accounts for $1.30/4.20 = 31$ percent; and all other sources explain $1.23/4.20 = 29$ percent. Substituting the data into (3), we find that $0.46/1.70 = 27$ percent of the growth in output per man-hour is explained by the increase in the ratio of material capital to labor, and $1.24/1.70 = 73$ percent is attributable to all other sources.

These calculations are, at best, suitable only for establishing relative orders of magnitude. For full discussions of imperfections in the data, see the works by Kendrick and Budd cited above. For a penetrating survey of the theoretical reservations to which such calculations are subject, see M. Ishaq Nadiri, "Some Approaches to the Theory and Measurement of Total Factor Productivity: A Survey," *Journal of Economic Literature*, VIII (Dec. 1970).

BIBLIOGRAPHY

The following books and articles range from simple descriptive accounts to highly sophisticated mathematical analyses, but all are informative and worth reading. No reference appears more than once, although many contributed to several chapters of this book.

CHAPTER I

Alchian, Armen A., "Uncertainty, Evolution, and Economic Theory," *Journal of Political Economy,* LX (June 1950).

———, "Information Costs, Pricing, and Resource Unemployment," *Western Economic Journal,* VII (June 1969).

———, and William R. Allen, *University Economics,* 2d ed. (Belmont, Calif.: Wadsworth, 1967).

Andreano, Ralph L., Ed., *The New Economic History: Recent Papers on Methodology* (New York: John Wiley and Sons, 1970).

Becker, Gary S., "Irrational Behavior and Economic Theory," *Journal of Political Economy,* LXX (Feb. 1962).

———, *Human Capital* (New York: National Bureau of Economic Research, 1964).

Dick, Trevor J. O., *An Economic Theory of Technological Change: The Case of Patents and United States Railroads, 1871–1950* (Unpublished doctoral dissertation, University of Washington, 1970).

Easterlin, Richard A., "Economic Growth," in *International Encyclopedia of the Social Sciences* (New York: Macmillan, 1968).

Fabricant, Solomon, "Productivity," in *International Encyclopedia of the Social Sciences* (New York: Macmillan, 1968).

Fischer, David Hackett, *Historians' Fallacies: Toward a Logic of Historical Thought* (New York: Harper and Row, 1970).

Fogel, Robert W., "The New Economic History: Its Findings and Methods," *Economic History Review,* XIX (Dec. 1966).

———, "The Specification Problem in Economic History," *Journal of Economic History,* XXVII (Sept. 1967).

Friedman, Milton, *Essays in Positive Economics* (Chicago: University of Chicago, 1953).

Hayek, Friederich A., "The Use of Knowledge in Society," *American Economic Review,* XXXV (Sept. 1945).

Hexter, J. H., "The Rhetoric of History," in *International Encyclopedia of the Social Sciences* (New York: Macmillan, 1968).

Johnson, H. G., "Towards a Generalized Capital Accumulation Approach to Economic Development," in M. Blaug, Ed., *Economics of Education 1: Selected Readings* (Baltimore: Penguin Books, 1968).

Kuhn, Thomas S., *The Structure of Scientific Revolutions,* 2d ed. (Chicago: University of Chicago, 1970).

Lipsey, Richard G., and Peter O. Steiner, *Economics,* 2d ed. (New York: Harper and Row, 1969).

Machlup, Fritz, "Patents," in *International Encyclopedia of the Social Sciences* (New York: Macmillan, 1968).

Meyer, John H., and Alfred H. Conrad, "Economic Theory, Statistical Inference, and Economic History," *Journal of Economic History,* XVII (Dec. 1957).

Morgenstern, Oskar, *On the Accuracy of Economic Observations,* 2d ed. (Princeton, N. J.: Princeton University, 1963).

Mortensen, Dale T., "Job Search, the Duration of Unemployment, and the Phillips Curve," *American Economic Review,* LX (Dec. 1970).

Nelson, Richard R., "The Economics of Invention: A Survey of the Literature," *Journal of Business,* XXXII (April 1959).

———, Ed., *The Rate and Direction of Inventive Activity* (Princeton, N. J.: Princeton University, 1962).

Popper, Karl R., *The Poverty of Historicism* (New York: Harper Torchbooks, 1964).

———, *The Logic of Scientific Discovery* (New York: Harper Torchbooks, 1965).

Rosenberg, Nathan, "Capital Goods, Technology, and Economic Growth," *Oxford Economic Papers,* XV (Nov. 1963).

Solow, Robert M., *Capital Theory and the Rate of Return* (Chicago: Rand McNally, 1965).

———, *Growth Theory* (New York: Oxford University, 1970).

Stigler, George J., "The Economics of Information," *Journal of Political Economy,* LXIX (June 1961).

———, "Information in the Labor Market," *Journal of Political Economy,* LXX (Supplement; Oct. 1962).

Young, Allyn, "Increasing Returns and Economic Progress," *Economic Journal,* XXXVIII (Dec. 1928).

CHAPTER II

Andreano, Ralph, Ed., *New Views on American Economic Development* (Cambridge, Mass.: Schenkman, 1965).

Barnett, Harold J., and Chandler Morse, *Scarcity and Growth: The Economics of Natural Resource Availability* (Baltimore: Johns Hopkins, 1963).

Becker, Gary S., "An Economic Analysis of Fertility," in National Bureau of Economic Research, *Demographic and Economic Change in Developed Countries* (Princeton, N. J.: Princeton University, 1960).

Brady, Dorothy, "Relative Prices in the Nineteenth Century," *Journal of Economic History,* XXIV (June 1964).

Camp, L. Sprague de, *The Heroic Age of American Invention* (Garden City, N. Y.: Doubleday, 1961).

Chandler, Alfred D., Jr., "The Beginnings of 'Big Business' in American Industry," *Business History Review,* XXXIII (Spring 1959).

———, *Strategy and Structure: Chapters in the History of Industrial Enterprise* (Cambridge, Mass.: M. I. T. Press, 1962).

Davis, Lance E., "The Investment Market, 1870–1914: The Evolution of a National Market," *Journal of Economic History,* XXV (Sept. 1965).

Denison, Edward F., "Some Major Issues in Productivity Analysis," *Survey of Current Business* (May 1969), Pt. II.

Evans, George Heberton, Jr., *Business Incorporations in the United States, 1800–1943* (New York: National Bureau of Economic Research, 1948).

Fishlow, Albert, "Levels of Nineteenth-Century Investment in Education," *Journal of Economic History,* XXVI (Dec. 1966).

———, "Productivity and Technological Change in the Railroad Sector," in National Bureau of Economic Research, Conference on Research in Income and Wealth, *Output, Employment, and Productivity in the United States after 1800* (New York: Columbia University, 1966).

Fogel, Robert William, *The Union Pacific Railroad* (Baltimore: Johns Hopkins, 1960).

———, *Railroads and American Economic Growth* (Baltimore: Johns Hopkins, 1964).

———, and Stanley L. Engerman, "A Model for the Explanation of Industrial Expansion during the Nineteenth Century: With an Application to the American Iron Industry," *Journal of Political Economy,* LXXVII (May/June 1969).

Friedman, Milton, and Anna J. Schwartz, *A Monetary History of the United States, 1867–1960* (Princeton, N. J.: Princeton University, 1963).

Gallman, Robert E., "Commodity Output, 1839–1899," in National Bureau of Economic Research, Conference on Research in Income and Wealth, *Trends in the American Economy in the Nineteenth Century* (Princeton, N. J.: Princeton University, 1960).

———, "Gross National Product in the United States, 1834–1909," in National Bureau of Economic Research, Conference on Research in Income and Wealth, *Output, Employment, and Productivity in the United States after 1800* (New York: Columbia University, 1966).

Hill, Peter J., *The Economic Impact of Immigration into the United States* (Unpublished doctoral dissertation, University of Chicago, 1970).

Hoover, Ethel D., "Retail Prices after 1850," in National Bureau of Economic Research, Conference on Research in Income and Wealth, *Trends in the American Economy in the Nineteenth Century* (Princeton, N. J.: Princeton University, 1960).

Jewkes, John, David Sawers, and Richard Stillerman, *The Sources of Invention*, 2d ed. (New York: W. W. Norton, 1969).

Jorgenson, Dale, and Zvi Griliches, "The Explanation of Productivity Change," *Review of Economic Studies*, XXXIV (July 1967).

Kendrick, John W., *Productivity Trends in the United States* (Princeton, N. J.: Princeton University, 1961).

Kuznets, Simon, *Capital in the American Economy* (Princeton, N. J.: Princeton University, 1961).

———, and Ernest Rubin, *Immigration and the Foreign Born* (New York: National Bureau of Economic Research, 1954).

———, *et al.*, *Population Redistribution and Economic Growth, United States, 1870–1950*, 3 vols. (Philadelphia: American Philosophical Society, 1957–64).

Lebergott, Stanley, *Manpower in Economic Growth* (New York: McGraw-Hill, 1964).

———, "Labor Force and Employment, 1800–1960," in National Bureau of Economic Research, Conference on Research in Income and Wealth, *Output, Employment, and Productivity in the United States after 1800* (New York: Columbia University, 1966).

———, "United States Transport Advance and Externalities," *Journal of Economic History*, XXVI (Dec. 1966).

MacAvoy, Paul W., *The Economic Effects of Regulation: The Trunk-Line Railroad Cartels and the Interstate Commerce Commission before 1900* (Cambridge, Mass.: M. I. T. Press, 1965).

Martin, Edgar W., *The Standard of Living in 1860* (Chicago: University of Chicago, 1942).

McGee, John S., "Predatory Price Cutting: The Standard Oil (N. J.) Case," *Journal of Law and Economics*, I (Oct. 1958).

Nadiri, M. Ishaq, "Some Approaches to the Theory and Measurement of Total Factor Productivity: A Survey," *Journal of Economic Literature*, VIII (Dec. 1970).

North, Douglass C., *Growth and Welfare in the American Past* (Englewood Cliffs, N. J.: Prentice-Hall, 1966).

Rosenberg, Nathan, "Technological Change in the Machine Tool Industry, 1840–1910," *Journal of Economic History*, XXIII (Dec. 1963).

———, "Economic Development and the Transfer of Technology: Some Historical Perspectives," *Technology and Culture*, XI (Oct. 1970).

———, "The Direction of Technological Change: Inducement Mechanisms and Focusing Devices," *Economic Development and Cultural Change*, XVII (Oct. 1969).

Salter, W. E. G., *Productivity and Technical Change*, 2d ed. (Cambridge, England: Cambridge University, 1966).

Schmookler, Jacob, *Invention and Economic Growth* (Cambridge, Mass.: Harvard University, 1966).

Spann, Robert M., and Edward W. Erickson, "The Economics of Railroading: The Beginning of Cartelization and Regulation," *Bell Journal of Economics and Management Science*, I (Autumn 1970).

Stigler, George J., "The Division of Labor Is Limited by the Extent of the Market," *Journal of Political Economy*, LXI (June 1951).

———, "The Economies of Scale," *Journal of Law and Economics*, I (Oct. 1958).

Strassman, W. Paul, *Risk and Technological Innovation: American Manufacturing Methods during the Nineteenth Century* (Ithaca: Cornell University, 1959).

Sylla, Richard, "Federal Policy, Banking Market Structure, and Capital Mobilization in the United States, 1863–1913," *Journal of Economic History*, XXIX (Dec. 1969).

Temin, Peter, *Iron and Steel in Nineteenth Century America* (Cambridge, Mass.: M. I. T. Press, 1964).

Thomas, Robert Paul, "The Automobile Industry and Its Tycoon," *Explorations in Entrepreneurial History*, VI (Winter, 1969).

U. S. Bureau of the Census, *Historical Statistics of the United States, Colonial Times to 1957* (Washington: Government Printing Office, 1960).

———, *Long Term Economic Growth, 1860–1965* (Washington: Government Printing Office, 1966).

Williamson, Jeffrey G., "Consumer Behavior in the Nineteenth Century: Carroll D. Wright's Massachusetts Workers in 1875," *Explorations in Entrepreneurial History*, IV (Winter 1967).

Wrigley, E. A., *Population and History* (New York: McGraw-Hill, 1969).

DIGRESSION

Andreano, Ralph, Ed., *The Economic Impact of the American Civil War*, 2d ed. (Cambridge, Mass.: Schenkman, 1967).

Barzel, Yoram, "Investment, Scale, and Growth," *Journal of Political Economy*, LXXIX (March/April 1971).

Cheung, Steven N. S., "The Structure of a Contract and the Theory of a Non-exclusive Resource," *Journal of Law and Economics*, XIII (April 1970).

Commons, John R., *Legal Foundations of Capitalism* (New York: Macmillan, 1924).

David, Paul A., "The Growth of Real Product in the United States Before 1840: New Evidence, Controlled Conjectures," *Journal of Economic History*, XXVII (June 1967).

Davis, Lance, and Douglass North, "Institutional Change and American Economic Growth: A First Step Towards a Theory of Institutional Innovation," *Journal of Economic History*, XXX (Jan. 1970).

Demsetz, Harold, "The Exchange and Enforcement of Property Rights," *Journal of Law and Economics*, VII (Oct. 1964).

———, "Some Aspects of Property Rights," *Journal of Law and Economics*, IX (Oct. 1966).

———, "Toward a Theory of Property Rights," *American Economic Review*, LVII (May 1967).

Fei, John C. H., and Gustav Ranis, "Economic Development in Historical Perspective," *American Economic Review*, LIX (May 1969).

Hamilton, Alexander, John Jay, and James Madison, *The Federalist* (New York: Modern Library, n. d.).

Hicks, J. R., *A Theory of Economic History* (London: Oxford University, 1969).

Hurst, James Willard, *Law and the Conditions of Freedom in the Nineteenth-Century United States* (Madison, Wis.: University of Wisconsin, 1956).

———, *Law and Social Process in United States History* (Ann Arbor, Mich.: University of Michigan, 1960).

———, *The Legitimacy of the Business Corporation in the Law of the United States, 1780–1970* (Charlottesville, Va.: University of Virginia, 1970).

Kempin, Frederick G., Jr., *Legal History: Law and Social Change* (Englewood Cliffs, N. J.: Prentice-Hall, 1963).

Lewis, W. Arthur, *The Theory of Economic Growth* (London: George Allen and Unwin, 1955).

North, Douglass C., *The Economic Growth of the United States, 1790–1860* (Englewood Cliffs, N. J.: Prentice-Hall, 1961).

———, "Institutional Change and Economic Growth," *Journal of Economic History*, XXXI (March 1971).

———, and Robert Paul Thomas, "An Economic Theory of the Growth of the Western World," *Economic History Review*, XXIII (April 1970).

Parker, William N., and Franklee Whartenby, "The Growth of Output before 1840," in National Bureau of Economic Research, Conference on Research in Income and Wealth, *Trends in the American Economy in the Nineteenth Century* (Princeton, N. J.: Princeton University, 1960).

Weber, Max, *On Law in Economy and Society* (Cambridge, Mass.: Harvard University, 1954).

Weissman, Jacob, *Law in a Business Society* (Englewood Cliffs, N. J.: Prentice-Hall, 1964).

CHAPTER III

Berry, Brian J. L., and Chauncy D. Harris, "Central Place," in *International Encyclopedia of the Social Sciences* (New York: Macmillan, 1968).

Buchanan, James M., and William Craig Stubblebine, "Externality," *Economica*, XXIX (Nov. 1962).

Coase, Ronald, "The Problem of Social Cost," *Journal of Law and Economics*, III (Oct. 1960).

Feller, Irwin, "The Urban Location of United States Invention 1860–1910," *Explorations in Economic History*, VIII (Spring 1971).

Fisher, Irving, *Report on National Vitality: Its Wastes and Conservation* (Washington: Government Printing Office, 1909).

Higgs, Robert, "The Growth of Cities in a Midwestern Region, 1870–1900," *Journal of Regional Science*, IX (Dec. 1969).

———, "Central Place Theory and Regional Urban Hierarchies: An Empirical Note," *Journal of Regional Science*, X (Aug. 1970).

———, "American Inventiveness, 1870–1920," *Journal of Political Economy*, LXXIX (May/June 1971).

———, "Cities and Yankee Ingenuity, 1870–1920," in Kenneth T. Jackson and Stanley Schultz, Eds., *From Village to Metropolis: Essays on the City in America* (New York: Knopf, 1972).

Hoover, Edgar M., *The Location of Economic Activity* (New York: McGraw-Hill, 1948).

Hoyt, Homer, *One Hundred Years of Land Values in Chicago* (Chicago: University of Chicago, 1933).

Isard, Walter, *Location and Space-Economy* (Cambridge, Mass.: M. I. T. Press, 1956).

Lampard, Eric E., "The Evolving System of Cities in the United States: Urbanization and Economic Development," in H. S. Perloff and L. W. Wingo, Eds., *Issues in Urban Economics* (Baltimore: Johns Hopkins, 1968).

Losch, August, *The Economics of Location* (New Haven: Yale University, 1954).

Meeker, Edward F., *The Economics of Improving Health, 1850–1915* (Unpublished doctoral dissertation, University of Washington, 1970).

Pred, Allan R., *The Spatial Dynamics of U. S. Urban-Industrial Growth, 1800–1914* (Cambridge, Mass.: M. I. T. Press, 1966).

Ravenel, Mazyck P., Ed., *A Half Century of Public Health* (New York: American Public Health Association, 1921).

Simon, Herbert A., "Effects of Increased Productivity upon the Ratio of Urban to Rural Population," *Econometrica*, XV (Jan. 1947).

Smith, Stephen, *The City That Was* (New York: Frank Allaben, 1911).

Smolensky, Eugene, and Donald Ratajczak, "The Conception of Cities," *Explorations in Entrepreneurial History*, II (Winter 1965).

Sydenstricker, Edgar, *Health and Environment* (New York: McGraw-Hill, 1933).

Winslow, C.-E. A., *The Evolution and Significance of the Modern Public Health Campaign* (New Haven: Yale University, 1923).

CHAPTER IV

Agelasto, A. M., *et al.*, "The Cotton Situation," in U. S. Department of Agriculture, *Yearbook, 1921* (Washington: Government Printing Office, 1922).

Ball, C. R., *et al.*, "Wheat Production and Marketing," in U. S. Department of Agriculture, *Yearbook, 1921* (Washington: Government Printing Office, 1922).

Bateman, Fred, "Improvement in American Dairy Farming, 1850–1910: A Quantitative Analysis," *Journal of Economic History*, XXVIII (June 1968).

———, "Labor Inputs and Productivity in American Dairy Agriculture, 1850–1910," *Journal of Economic History*, XXIX (June 1969).

Bogue, Allan G., *Money at Interest: The Farm Mortgage on the Middle Border* (Ithaca, N. Y.: Cornell University, 1955).

———, *From Prairie to Corn Belt: Farming on the Illinois and Iowa Prairies in the Nineteenth Century* (Chicago: University of Chicago, 1963).

Bowman, John D., "An Economic Analysis of Midwestern Farm Land Values and Farm Land Income, 1860 to 1900," *Yale Economic Essays*, V (Fall 1965).

Cheung, Steven N. S., "Private Property Rights and Sharecropping," *Journal of Political Economy*, LXXVI (Nov./Dec. 1968).

———, "Transaction Costs, Risk Aversion, and the Choice of Contractual Arrangements," *Journal of Law and Economics*, XII (April 1969).

Fite, Gilbert C., "Daydreams and Nightmares: The Late Nineteenth-Century Agricultural Frontiers," *Agricultural History*, XL (Oct. 1966).

Fogel, Robert William, and Jack Rutner, "The Efficiency Effects of Federal Land Policy, 1850–1900: A Report of Some Provisional Findings," University of Chicago Center for Mathematical Studies in Business and Economics, Report 7027 (June 1970).

Hayami, Yujiro, and V. W. Ruttan, "Factor Prices and Technical Change in Agricultural Development: The United States and Japan, 1880–1960," *Journal of Political Economy*, LXXVIII (Sept./Oct. 1970).

Higgs, Robert, "Railroad Rates and the Populist Uprising," *Agricultural History*, XLIV (July 1970).

Leighty, C. E., *et. al.*, "The Corn Crop," in U. S. Department of Agriculture, *Yearbook, 1921* (Washington: Government Printing Office, 1922).

Lerner, Eugene M., "Southern Output and Agricultural Income, 1860–1880," *Agricultural History*, XXXIII (July 1959).

Nugent, Walter T. K., "Some Parameters of Populism," *Agricultural History*, XL (Oct. 1966).

Parker, William N., and Judith L. V. Klein, "Productivity Growth in Grain Production in the United States, 1840–60 and 1900–10," in National Bureau of Economic Research, Conference on Research in Income and Wealth, *Output, Employment, and Productivity in the United States after 1800* (New York: Columbia University, 1966).

Parker, William N., "Sources of Agricultural Productivity in the Nineteenth Century," *Journal of Farm Economics*, IL (Dec. 1967).

Rasmussen, Wayne D., "The Impact of Technological Change on American Agriculture, 1862–1962," *Journal of Economic History*, XXII (Dec. 1962).

Rogin, Leo, *The Introduction of Farm Machinery in its Relation to the Productivity of Labor in the Agriculture of the United States During the Nineteenth Century* (Berkeley: University of California, 1931).

Rothstein, Morton, "America in the International Rivalry for the British Wheat Market," *Mississippi Valley Historical Review*, XLVII (Dec. 1960).

Russell, E. Z., *et al.*, "Hog Production and Marketing," in U. S. Department of Agriculture, *Yearbook, 1922* (Washington: Government Printing Office, 1923).

Sheets, E. W., *et al.*, "Our Beef Supply," in U. S. Department of Agriculture, *Yearbook, 1921* (Washington: Government Printing Office, 1922).

Strauss, Frederick, and Louis H. Bean, *Gross Farm Income and Indices of Farm Production and Prices in the United States, 1869–1937*, U. S. Department of Agriculture, Technical Bulletin 703, 1940.

Tostlebe, Alvin S., *Capital in Agriculture: Its Formation and Financing since 1870* (Princeton, N. J.: Princeton University, 1957).

CHAPTER V

Abramovitz, Moses, "The Welfare Interpretation of Secular Trends in National Income and Product," in Moses Abramovitz, *et al., The Allocation of Economic Resources* (Stanford: Stanford University, 1959).

Becker, Gary S., *The Economics of Discrimination* (Chicago: University of Chicago, 1957).

Budd, Edward C., "Factor Shares, 1850–1910," in National Bureau of Economic Research, Conference on Research in Income and Wealth, *Trends in the American Economy in the Nineteenth Century* (Princeton, N. J.: Princeton University, 1960).

Davis, Lance, "Capital Immobilities and Finance Capitalism: A Study of Economic Evolution in the United States, 1820–1920," *Explorations in Entrepreneurial History*, I (Fall 1963).

Easterlin, Richard A., "Interregional Differences in Per Capita Income, Population, and Total Income, 1840–1950," in National Bureau of Economic Research, Conference on Research in Income and Wealth, *Trends in the American Economy in the Nineteenth Century* (Princeton, N. J.: Princeton University, 1960).

———, "Regional Income Trends, 1840–1950," in Seymour E. Harris, Ed., *American Economic History* (New York: McGraw-Hill, 1961).

Engerman, Stanley L., "The Economic Impact of the Civil War," *Explorations in Entrepreneurial History*, III (Spring/Summer 1966).

Fels, Rendigs, *American Business Cycles, 1865–1897* (Chapel Hill, N. C.: University of North Carolina, 1959).

Gallman, Robert E., "Trends in the Size Distribution of Wealth in the Nineteenth Century: Some Speculations," in National Bureau of Economic Research, Conference on Research in Income and Wealth, *Six Papers on the Size Distribution of Wealth and Income* (New York: Columbia University, 1969).

Hayes, Marion, "A Century of Change: Negroes in the U. S. Economy, 1860–1960," *Monthly Labor Review*, LXXXV (Dec. 1962).

Higgs, Robert, "Race, Skills, and Earnings: American Immigrants in 1909," *Journal of Economic History*, XXXI (June 1971).

Hourwich, Isaac A., *Immigration and Labor: The Economic Aspects of European Immigration to the United States* (New York: G. P. Putnam's Sons, 1912).

Lebergott, Stanley, "Wage Trends, 1800–1900," in National Bureau of Economic Research, Conference on Research in Income and Wealth, *Trends in the American Economy in the Nineteenth Century* (Princeton, N. J.: Princeton University, 1960).

Long, Clarence D., *Wages and Earnings in the United States, 1860–1890* (Princeton, N. J.: Princeton University, 1960).

Mishan, E. J., "The Postwar Literature on Externalities: An Interpretative Essay," *Journal of Economic Literature*, IX (March 1971).

———, *The Costs of Economic Growth* (New York: Frederick A. Praeger, 1967).

Nourse, Hugh O., *Regional Economics* (New York: McGraw-Hill, 1968).

Olson, Mancur, Jr., "Rapid Growth as a Destabilizing Force," *Journal of Economic History*, XXIII (Dec. 1963).

Perloff, Harvey S., *et al.*, *Regions, Resources, and Economic Growth* (Baltimore: Johns Hopkins, 1960).

Rees, Albert, *Real Wages in Manufacturing, 1890–1914* (Princeton, N. J.: Princeton University, 1961).

Sjaastad, Larry, "The Costs and Returns of Human Migration," *Journal of Political Economy*, LXX (Supplement; Oct. 1962).

Solmon, Lewis C., "Estimates of the Costs of Schooling in 1880 and 1890," *Explorations in Economic History*, VII (Supplement; 1970).

———, "Opportunity Costs and Models of Schooling in the Nineteenth Century," *Southern Economic Journal*, XXXVII (July 1970).

Soltow, Lee C., "Evidence on Income Inequality in the United States, 1866–1965," *Journal of Economic History*, XXIX (June 1969).

INDEX